OPERA GUIDE **43**

Frontispiece: 'Oedipus Rex' at Sadler's Wells, 1960: producer, Michel Saint Denis; designer, Abd'Elkader Farrah. (photo: David Sims)

This Opera Guide is sponsored by

43

Oedipus Rex
The Rake's Progress

Igor Stravinsky

Opera Guide Series Editor: Nicholas John

John
Ri

Publi·   ·n National Opera

CONTENTS

LIST OF ILLUSTRATIONS

Cover design by Anita Boyd; photograph of Stravinsky by Laelia Goehr.
Frontispiece: *Oedipus Rex* at Sadler's Wells, 1960. (photo: David Sims)

Picture research: Ian Stones

The Person of Fate and the Fate of the Person: Stravinsky's 'Oedipus Rex'

David Nice

Behold, spectator . . . one of the most perfect machines constructed by the infernal gods for the mathematical annihilation of a mortal.
Cocteau, Prologue to Act One of *The Infernal Machine*, 1934

My audience is not indifferent to the fate of the person, but I think it far more concerned with the person of the fate, and the delineation of it which can be achieved uniquely in music.
Stravinsky to Robert Craft in *Dialogues and a Diary*, 1963

Caught between the snares of Stravinsky and Cocteau, what chance does Oedipus the man have of holding his head above circumstances? In Sophocles' tragedy, there is a kind of double consciousness at work: the gods have already set the trap, Oedipus has killed his father and married his mother, but everything he does within the course of the play, he does as a free agent, and most often from the highest motives. He is the one to ask the questions, to lose his temper when answers point the finger in an unexpected direction, and to steer back on course in a quest which will bring everything into the light. Cocteau seems to have given him little credit for an inquiring mind. His Oedipus is a king of cards who has to suffer before he learns anything. In *The Infernal Machine* — a salvage-job on everything Stravinsky forced him to pare away in *Oedipus Rex* — we see a power-hungry youth charging across the Freudian red lights into a marriage with a woman old enough to be his mother (not an aspect of the myth which bothered Sophocles). What remains of the archetypal tyrant in the libretto of *Oedipus Rex* could easily have given Stravinsky the cue for the kind of monumental impersonation of a tragedy which Constant Lambert, among others, took it to be.

Yet this opera-oratorio, apparently frozen in set numbers, lends its king a heart long before the awful truth dawns. Discussing *Oedipus Rex* nearly forty years later, Stravinsky with characteristic caution placed inverted commas around the 'heart', but for an audience caught up in the cogs of the action, it ought to be apparent without them. In the cold light of examination, there are many layers to peel away before we can come to the same conclusion, drawing an equation which brings together Stravinsky and Verdi. The layers are the 'constraints', as Stravinsky called them, which he imposed only to give himself a greater freedom of expression within bounds. The inner layer is made up of the references to just about every operatic precedent under the sun, some in ironic quotation-marks and others which match the reference with reverence (we shall want to know why, for example, Oedipus's aria of reproach to Tiresias seems 'sincere' to us, whereas Creon's declamation does not; for both are tributes to the past, stamped with the character of Stravinsky). The outer layer is the rigorous framework, the governing style of the piece, which seems to have preoccupied Stravinsky to the exclusion of all else at the start of every project.

In the case of *Oedipus Rex*, his touchstone was the use of cast-iron Latin as the language of tragedy. It is the first sticking-point for those who see in the work only an insistent austerity, and Stravinsky's commendation, in his autobiography, of 'a medium not dead, but turned to stone, and so monumentalized as to have become immune from all risk of vulgarization',

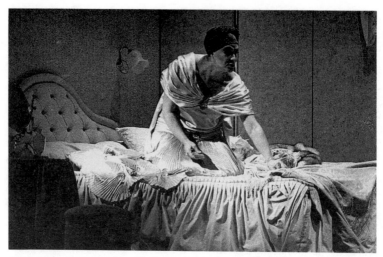

Giorgio Marini's production with Lucia Valentini-Terrani as Jocasta, La Fenice, 1989. (photo: Arici & Smith)

needs careful qualifying. Stopping over in Genoa on the way from Venice to Nice in September 1925, Stravinsky found in a bookseller's a copy of Joergensen's *Life of St Francis of Assisi*. What struck him was the fact that the saint used Provençal for solemn occasions rather than his everyday Italian; he, too, was looking for a special language in his next work, which he had already decided would carry hieratical overtones and which would be set for larger forces than any he had employed in the other so-called 'neo-classical' works of the 1920s (curiously enough, he had already used an old French text for an unfinished work of the previous year, *A Dialogue between Joy and Reason*). We should also take into account his new-found religious sensibility; that same September, an abscess on his right forefinger healed shortly after a prayer offered before a 'miraculous' icon in Nice (Stravinsky's inverted commas again). The first phase of his Christian orthodoxy dates from this period.

The immediate result, however, was no mass or *Symphony of Psalms* (written three years later than *Oedipus*, with which it has more than a little in common), but an 'archetypal drama of purification', and Stravinsky chose the Oedipus myth as a subject which would be universally familiar; no one need worry too much about the words. Moreover, he told Robert Craft in 1963 that he used Latin rather than Sophocles' Greek 'because I had no notion of how to treat Greek musically (or Latin, Latinists will say, but there I did at least have *my* idea)'. *His* idea, as it turned out, was to dissect the word and 'treat' the syllable as the music dictated, regardless of stress or sense, and to take the setting of language still further away from the Wagnerian enslavement of the music to the word, already dismantled in his idiosyncratic use of Russian in *Les Noces* (1914-17) and the slavic 'opera-buffa' *Mavra* (1923). Engaged on the composition of *Oedipus* in 1925, he wrote:

> In my *Oedipus Rex*, the word is pure material, functioning musically like a block of marble or stone in a work of sculpture or architecture. *Oedipus* represents a great advance on [*Les Noces*], for while the musical work that uses a living contemporary language has many elements that evoke emotion and sentiments in us, the language destroys the words as pure

musical material. For this reason, the use of a dead language is justified . . .

Once or twice, Stravinsky found himself in trouble with the Latinists; one scholar pointed out that the setting of 'cecidi' with a stress over the first syllable rather than the second would read 'a king fell Laius' rather than 'a king slew Laius'. He altered the rhythm for 'Ego senem cecidi' (but not for 'Rex cecidit Laium'). He accented with a conscious freedom to such an extent that the very pronunciation of the name 'Oedipus' fluctuates at will. None of this, however, should imply that Stravinsky ignored the expressive potential of any given speech at any point in the text.

It seems a far cry, all the same, from his diligent work on the English libretto for *The Rake's Progress* over twenty years later. There he had for the first time a poet, in W.H. Auden, who shared his views; it was a collaboration of the highest order. The same could hardly be said of his relationship with André Gide, who found to his dismay that his French text for *Perséphone* (1933) had been stretched and 'treated' out of all recognition, nor yet of Cocteau —though there at least the violence was done to a libretto which, after severe shredding, had been handed over to the priest (later Cardinal) Jean Daniélou for translation into Latin. It was, no doubt, a disappointment to Cocteau after the brighter hopes of earlier years. Stravinsky and Cocteau had met under the aegis of Diaghilev's Ballets Russes in the spring of 1910, and the première of *The Rite of Spring* three years later impressed Cocteau as 'the very image of artistic rebellion'. Eager to jump on the progressive bandwagon and to provide another shockable triumph for Diaghilev, he proposed to Stravinsky the idea of a ballet on the subject of David — a kind of old testament cabaret set in a fairground booth — though that came to nothing probably because Stravinsky lacked all interest in the subject ('I think David was biblical', he remarked drily at a later date, 'and at that time I avoided anything biblical').

Stravinsky's curiosity revived, however, when he saw Sophocles' *Antigone* set to the rhythm of the 'twenties in Cocteau's 1923 adaptation (whilst working on *Oedipus Rex*, he must have liked *Orphée* too, for he later singled out Heurtebise, the glazier angel with wings of glass, as his favourite Cocteau character). He may well have chosen Cocteau as a collaborator for his striking visual sense — so vital in the setting of *Oedipus Rex* as a one-dimensional opera-oratorio — since the first draft of the text was not to his liking ('a music drama in meretricious prose' was the 1963 verdict), and he came to loathe the few remnants of authentic Cocteau left in the final version, namely the Speaker's narrative between the scenes.

Cocteau was not, in fact, to take any kind of centre stage in the *Oedipus* partnership. His talents for design were not employed in the première, a concert performance rather than a production owing to shortage of time (and Stravinsky remarked that it fared badly indeed following a fully-staged performance of *The Firebird*). Nor did Diaghilev repay with much thanks this top-secret birthday present for the twentieth birthday of the Ballets Russes; the role of the Speaker, which Cocteau certainly envisaged as his own, went to a handsome younger man. His time was yet to come: in 1952, at the Théâtre des Champs-Élysées, he took double credit as actor and designer, fashioning a number of weird and wonderful masks and producing several 'apparitions'. In these mimes between the music, he found a place for many of the phantasmagorical creatures and sacred monsters which people the much broader canvas of *The Infernal Machine*. Stravinsky, who conducted those extraordinary performances, at first expressed reservations that the *tableaux vivants* would undermine the nature of his opera-oratorio, but he ended up giving them his blessing.

In 1927, though, Cocteau's stage directions were rigid indeed. Everything was to take place on one level, with no hint of perspectives, and the chorus was to stand in lines, 'concealed behind a kind of bas-relief in three ascending tiers. Except for Tiresias, the Shepherd and the Messenger, the characters remain in their built-up costumes and in their masks. Only their arms and heads move. They should give the impression of living statues.' In this stony setting, and through the stony medium of the Latin language, the person of fate prepares to crush its already half-petrified subjects to death.

And that, it seems, was indeed Stravinsky's starting-point, though as he progressed with composition of the work in strict chronological order, he was able to bring what he called his 'manners' to bear on the human beings caught in the trap. The first sketch in his notebook, however, was the *ostinato* triplet figure for harp, piano and timpani which beats softly but insistently against the Chorus's 'Oedipus, Oedipus, adest pestis' [2]. Its interval of a minor third casts a shadow across the whole work, first as the two central notes of the four-note theme which underpins the chorus's opening gesture [1], and it returns whenever Stravinsky wants to turn the screw of fate. Creon's empty C major proclamation that Thebes will be saved from the plague if Laius's murderer can be discovered turns to F minor as he reveals that the culprit is hidden in the city; the minor third interval launches the clarinet arpeggio against 'Latet peremptor'. C major raucously reasserts itself, but reverts to the minor for Oedipus's response [5] (the minor third again on 'Non, non'). Tension rises a notch as the Chorus prays to the Gods, guides of the infernal machine, to uncover the malefactor at the beginning of the next scene; as the Speaker outlines the action to come, the music grinds upwards from Oedipus's newly-confident E flat major ('Clarissimus Oedipus, polliceor divinabo' — 'I, far-

David Hockney, 'Raised Stage with Masks, Narrator and Auditorium for "Oedipus Rex"', gouache and tempera, 1981. (photo: David Hockney)

10

famed Oedipus, will discover the guilty one') to B minor, and the *ostinato* [2] returns on harp, piano and timpani as before, softly reinforced this time by cellos and basses. Tiresias's reluctance to tell what he knows [7] has the bassoon stuck in a groove before it hits the third note of the minor scale and climbs upwards, but when Oedipus accuses Tiresias of the murder, he brings the truth into the open and the minor thirds sound openly again on 'dicam'. Oedipus's reply [8] returns to E flat major, more vulnerable this time, but dies into the almost unbearable C minor hopelessness of 'volunt regem perire', a keening repetition of the minor third (marked *doloroso* — one of several tell-tale expressive markings in the score).

After the harshly brilliant C major contrast of the central 'Gloria' chorus [9], we are plunged back into troubled intimacy, this time for Jocasta's scene, soft and slightly pathetic at first as scored for flute and harp; although Stravinsky does not observe the repeat of the 'Gloria' in his live 1952 recording from the Théâtre des Champs-Élysées, he was later to stress how important it is to hear it again, since the Chorus cadences on G major, and Jocasta's music begins in G minor. So there is a perfect symmetry at the mid-point of the piece between public pomp and private doubts (those of Oedipus followed by those of Jocasta). The Queen's reprimands are regal yet riddled with foreboding; the minor third accompanies her rather sensual 'Nonn' erubescite' [10] on harp and timpani, before passing into the voice for the obsessive rhythms of 'Oracula, oracula' [11]. Jocasta is saying that she does not believe in oracles but her music tells us otherwise (which is rather close to the music-drama methods Stravinsky professed to despise). Much later, as the Messenger arrives to announce the Queen's death, trumpets hammer out the minor third in yet another fate-laden pattern before swivelling upwards into hollow major fanfares [17]. Oedipus's steady discovery of the truth makes further play on

'Oedipus Rex' at the National Theatre, Belgrade, 1967. (photo: Miroslav Krstig)

tense rhythms employing the minor third in the fast-heartbeat timpani semiquavers in groups of six as he tells Jocasta that he has killed an old man at the crossroads, and in the string and clarinet ricochets which effectively silence the flutes' last glimmers of light just before 'Lux facta est'. As the Chorus gently drives the blind king into exile at the end of the work, the *ostinato* [2] returns in its barest form — on timpani, cellos and double-basses — to have the last word.

Yet Oedipus and Jocasta, caught between fate and the red-carpet treatment, are not quite as helpless as that brief survey might make them seem. The king is a puppet, unable to ask the kind of intelligent questions that Sophocles puts into his mouth, but he is alive in the way that Petrushka is alive, and Stravinsky lends him a measure of pathos. We certainly see more of him than we do of those two Stravinskian characters who seal their fate with half-open eyes, the soldier in *The Soldier's Tale* or weak Tom Rakewell in *The Rake's Progress*. Note that in those remarks of Stravinsky's which preface this piece, he only said that his audience was *far more* concerned with the person of the fate — it was not indifferent to the fate of the person. As always in the so-called neo-classical works, and even in *Petrushka*, Stravinsky claims sympathy obliquely: remember that the head and arms of Oedipus are still free to move. And he is certainly not Cocteau's arrogant king.

Look first at the beginning of the aria 'Invidia fortunam odit', which Stravinsky in 1963 called (and without further elaboration) the key to the 'manner question' [8]. In the play, Oedipus's irrational response to Tiresias's charge shows him in his least flattering aspect, and Cocteau's text continues its character-assassination. Stravinsky's setting, however, is much warmer than the context might suggest. Surely this opening phrase reminds us of Verdi's *Requiem* — where the tenor plays the suppliant before God in the E*b* major section of the 'Ingemisco'.

Stravinsky

Verdi *Requiem*

The key and the vocal compass are the same; Verdi marks the line to be sung *dolce con calma* and Stravinsky's Oedipus is to sing *p tranquillo e ben cantando*. No less interesting are the differences: Stravinsky's line is elliptical by the side of Verdi's and, instead of rising to the E*b* at the end of Verdi's phrase, Oedipus cuts off tersely at the lowest note. It also contains, in the portion of the phrase marked *x*, the same melismatic writing which characterised Oedipus at his first entry [3], where we were tempted to trace it back to anything from Monteverdi up to Mozartian *opera seria* (it may be far-fetched to describe it, like Roman Vlad, as a musical illustration of 'vanity and weakness'; though that, of course, will depend on whether the tenor really sings it in the restrained *bel canto* style it demands). Leonard Bernstein, however, made the most fascinating connection of all in the sixth of his Harvard Lectures; with Verdi again, and Amneris's pleas for mercy as the priests condemn Radamès to death in Act Four scene one of *Aida*. His explicit comparison was between the anguished diminished seventh when Oedipus cries 'Creo vult munus regis' in this aria and Amneris's 'Ah, pietà!'.

Stravinsky *Oedipus Rex*

Verdi *Aida*

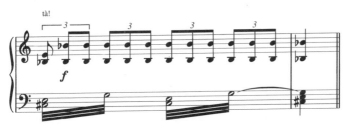

Bernstein went further: what about those seminal four notes at the start of *Oedipus Rex* [1] and Aida's entreaties to Amneris earlier in the Verdi opera? The situations are, of course, the same: a subject begs royalty for mercy, and royalty will itself soon be begging a higher authority for mercy.

This may sound like an irrelevant game of spot-the-reference, were it not for a few clues left by Stravinsky. Talking about *Oedipus* in 1963, he tersely remarked that 'if another composer is suggested in my score, he is Verdi'. And that is that. But here is Stravinsky writing in 1935:

> Verdi! Verdi! The great mighty Verdi! How many beautiful things there are in his early works as well as in the final ones. I admire him unconditionally, a truly great composer: I prefer Verdi to all other music of the nineteenth century.

And that would seem to include Tchaikovsky, the source of inspiration for his 1928 ballet *Le Baiser de la fée (The Fairy's Kiss)* and joint dedicatee, with Glinka and Pushkin, of *Mavra*. Stravinsky's other musical gods all stood behind many of the finest 'neo-classical' works; the greater the debt, the more original the work. The simple secret might be summed up in the composer's retort to accusations of disrespect in his treatment of Pergolesi as a source for the ballet *Pulcinella*: '*You* respect, *I* love'. So it was with Tchaikovsky and Verdi. In his 1939-40 Harvard Lectures, Stravinsky singles out the thunderstorm in *Rigoletto* as praiseworthy:

> He did not hesitate to make use of a formula which many a composer had employed before him. Verdi applies his own inventiveness to it and, without going outside of the tradition, makes out of a commonplace a perfectly original page that bears his unmistakable mark.

In quite a different way, many of Stravinsky's 'perfectly original pages' build on a number of Verdian formulas which were far from commonplace in the first place.

Even so, Oedipus is far from a Verdian hero for all occasions; only think of the all-too-regular metrical thrashing with which he tries to brave the truth implicit in the speeches of the Shepherd and Messenger — what Stravinsky tellingly called the 'Beckmesser aria', 'Nonne monstrum' [15] — or the utterly spare, simple moment of truth, 'Lux facta est' [16], which makes use only of the simplest elements in musical vocabulary to unforgettable effect. Stravinsky shows a careful sympathy in the score-markings: the dotted semiquaver figures which preface Oedipus's address to the people are *espressivo*, the four solo cellos in his second solo of scene one are to be played *dolce, cantabile* and full strings make a lean but telling contribution to 'Invidia fortunam'. (After a long period where acid combinations of brass and woodwind had been uppermost in Stravinsky's music, he was to exploit the singing qualities of the string department in his next work on a classical subject, *Apollo* — all white light after the enveloping darkness of *Oedipus Rex*.) It is important, too, to note that Oedipus should be sung 'not . . . by a large operatic voice, but a lyrical one.' Peter Pears in the earlier of his two recordings, with the composer conducting, surely comes closest to the ideal.

Other 'manners' in the score correspond perfectly with the different points in the drama. Creon's hollow confidence is decked out with the empty clichés of the eighteenth- and early-nineteenth-century mass [4a, 4b], their banality

14

underlined here by trombone and piccolo clarinet. One wonders, too, what Stravinsky made of the 'Gloria' in Beethoven's *Missa Solemnis* (he described the return of the ascending theme in Creon's aria in terms reminiscent of the Folies Bergères: 'The girls enter, kicking.') His 'Gloria' echoes Mussorgsky's *Boris Godunov* —public acclaim set against private suffering again — as well as Russian church ritual; and the Messenger seems to bring a whiff of pagan Russia to one of the few sections in the opera where Stravinsky returns to the more complex rhythms of earlier works [13].

By this stage in the tragedy, Stravinsky achieves his own brand of pity and terror, half-ironic and half-deadly, with more fixed metres: the 'Keystone Cops' music for the panicky duet of Oedipus and Jocasta [12], for example, or the 6/8 chromatic stamping of the Chorus at the news of Jocasta's death [18], which Stravinsky called a 'mortuary tarantella'. The regularity throughout is the composer's tribute to Sophocles' Greek metres: where many of the original choruses are in 3/8, Stravinsky corresponds with 6/8. That was yet another concession to the letter of the Greek tragedy; as for the spirit, embodied in the balance between the person of fate and the fate of Oedipus as a living, breathing character, he came closer to the world of Sophocles than Cocteau ever envisaged.

Patricia Johnson as Jocasta, Sadler's Wells

Cocteau staged his French version of the Sophocles tragedy, with Jean Marais as Oedipus and with costumes by Coco Chanel, at the Théâtre Antoine, Paris, 1937. (photo: Roger-Viollet)

Paris, 1952. Stravinsky with Cocteau at a rehearsal for the Théâtre des Champs-Elysées production. (photo: Roger-Viollet)

'Oedipus Rex': A Personal View

Judith Weir

When I first heard *Oedipus Rex*, in the sixties or the beginning of the seventies, new music was in a confused state. It lacked clarity; and to come across this score full of clear melody and harmony and structures was extraordinary. What is more, dramatically speaking, and again because of that absolute clarity, it is unique; I can't think of a bolder piece. It is very caught up in the story-telling, and in the tragedy, and yet there is something comic about the presentation which never fails to raise a smile.

Sometimes this is quite outrageous. For instance, when Jocasta says, 'Oracles are all wrong because Laius was killed at a cross-roads,' and Oedipus says, 'Well, come to think of it, I once killed an old man at a cross-roads,' it is almost absurdist theatre, almost Ionesco. Or when the 'nuntius horribilis' ('the messenger with dread tidings') comes in, there is the shock of hearing a language that we associate with solemnity spoken conversationally. The Narrator may say that he wishes to preserve a certain monumental aspect in the story, and for Stravinsky the value of a dead language may have been to distance the action from the audience, but in fact its almost conversational quality is fascinating. After the prophecy is revealed, Jocasta remarks 'Nonn' erubescite' ('Are you not ashamed'). My impression of classical Latin is that the sentences are very long, and a lot of time can be spent looking for the verb that will make sense of them! Here the phrases are short, like an Italian opera libretto, and the language comes across as a sort of ancient Italian, with an extraordinary immediacy.

If you had to explain dramatic irony to a visitor from Mars, you would choose this story, and this version especially. Oedipus knows everything except the one thing which, because of the Prologue, the audience knows. The text dwells upon this. When Oedipus at last realises the truth — 'Lux facta est' (literally, 'All is brought to light') — there is the additional irony that he is about to put out his own eyes. Some people might find this too simple but I find it absolutely enthralling to have these points underlined. Stravinsky gives the flute an unusual figure and sets the syllables in exactly equal quantities, as he also did with semibreves on Creon's line 'Tebis peremptor latet' ('the murderer is hiding in Thebes'). Just a few simple notes, almost no notes at all... It is a very anti-dramatic way of setting the lines, and yet it is monumental and mysterious. Just before 'Lux facta est' comes the magnificent passage when Oedipus is grasping what has happened: the strings shudder, and there is a light chord of three flutes, two right at the top. After the shudders it is absolutely still. Fanfares follow, when we might have expected a large chorus; instead the trumpets further raise expectation, rather like a call-sign on the radio — perhaps the music to express the events is unimaginable. Stravinsky never sets words as you would expect.

I never get tired of the freshness of the narrative technique. There is something exciting and sinister about the language of the prologues themselves. I remember 'trivium, crossroads, the place where three roads meet' from the first time I heard it. The composer intends us to know exactly what is going on, and the repetition of the story is certainly not boring. In this most famous of stories, it further underlines the irony.

*

What really interests me about the music of *Oedipus Rex* is the way that Stravinsky keeps little groups of instruments in very narrow wavebands. Even for him, this must be among the most clinically precise of scores. His attention to register is extraordinary, and he uses some very extreme registers exclusively, careful not to cover the tenor or baritone voices with orchestral sound. Each instrument group operates at a different height in the score (the woodwind are usually right at the top), and the voices are in between. Whether this makes for a static effect depends on the harmony. Often the harmony *is* very directional, much more so than most harmony in this century, and constantly moving towards cadences. Just look at the opening chorus, with piano, harp, timpani and low strings playing low notes; the harmony is at times standing around in thirds — 'e peste serva nos' ('save us from the plague') — but the whole chorus is nevertheless in a clear B♭ minor, striding confidently from tonic to dominant.

Stravinsky articulates the drama all the time through the orchestra. An obvious example is when the whole chorus starts singing 'trivium' over a chord on harp, timpani, piano, and four-part *pizzicato* cellos. This brittle sound immediately tells us that something is afoot. The orchestra is not as large as that in *The Rite of Spring*, of course, but it is triple woodwind, and it is always finding new instruments to say something new about the action.

A characteristic of *Oedipus Rex* is the terrific engine which rushes through the score, carrying the words along with a motor rhythm. For me, it is most like basic Italian opera, with its persistent rhythmic dynamo in 12/8 and 6/8, and clean, piercingly-pitched vocal lines. This is ideally demonstrated on Abbado's recording, where the singing is freely lyrical and dramatic; this, alas, isn't always the case with Stravinsky performances. For instance at Jocasta's aria 'Oracula mentiuntur' ('The oracles lie'), Abbado's tempo is fast, with rhythmic figures exaggerated to the point of (intentional) absurdity; the orchestral sound, with its ludicrously high clarinets and piccolo, could be the fastest bit of a Rossini overture.

When the drama begins to hot up with the revelations of the Shepherd and the Messenger, the music calms down for one of the least tense passages in the whole piece. Stravinsky allows the motor to run down, and then speeds up in each of the succeeding scenes.

*

I have been fascinated by the narrative technique. Because the first scene in the play, when Thebes is seen suffering from the plague, is cut, the audience must undertand this from what the Narrator says. Just once his speech merges into the music, with the oracular pronouncement: 'He who kills the king is a king'). But Stravinsky does not pursue the relationship of spoken and half-sung text in the way that Berg demands in *Wozzeck*. The characters deliver their words almost as though it is merely a script.

The music for Oedipus changes from scene to scene. His voice makes its first entry *dolce ma ben articulato* and continues to be (often surprisingly) lyrical. On the whole, Stravinsky doesn't use vocal style to tell us that Oedipus is a man of action and of overweening ambition: it is the story and the text which inform us of this. Perhaps the effect, in the end, is to humanise his plight; a great atmosphere of sympathy towards him inflates in the final pages. We feel sympathy because we know what is going to happen.

Creon's aria is very Italianate. When he quotes the oracle, we hear the strangely remote tone-colour of the E♭ clarinet, vulgar, yet cold and clinical. Incidentally, it is amusing how the characters consider the oracle to be just as unreliable as any other source of information — when Jocasta remarks that oracles lie, she is not wrong, any more than she is desperate to change the subject. The chorus interventions are also reminiscent of Verdi, and the general mood is quite relaxed, building up to the entry of Tiresias.

Tiresias sings in a low register, down to F#. Nowadays you might imagine he would be cast as a countertenor. At first Tiresias is accompanied by the thinnest of textures; a two-part invention for violins and bassoon. As the implications of his words mount up, so does the orchestration. Oedipus responds almost snakily; when he rages he stops singing altogether: 'Stipendarius es, Tiresias' ('You are his accomplice, Tiresias').

It's a bit confusing that Act One ends focused upon this confrontation; Oedipus' quarrel with Creon is only referred to very briefly here (compared with its significance in the original play). The preceding narrative promises that we will see Oedipus 'accuse Creon of wanting the throne' but this argument only takes the form of a passing remark to Tiresias. This is perhaps a function of the piece's dramatic mechanism whereby no character except Oedipus is allowed back to sing on a second occasion! Creon has sung his bit, and now it is Tiresias who happens to be in the firing line. It's a strange way to plan an opera but it has the effect of focusing the progression of events in the most extreme way possible. Notice the careful choices Stravinsky made in the orchestration of the first Act's final chorus: the timpani and the piano, used very much as a percussive instrument, are right at the bottom — dry as dust — while the horns are extremely high. And then, just after Jocasta's entrance, there are wonderful chords as though someone had sat down at a cocktail piano... Jocasta creates an effect, of course, because she has the only woman's voice in the opera but oddly enough her first entrance is quite classical; the beautiful cadences on 'altercationibus' ('strife') into E♭ minor remind me of Bach. The music slips into a slow Bellini-esque movement, which is stately and rather sinister.

Jocasta alternates between two tempi: the slow pace gives way to a histrionic section in 2/2, a very fast tempo, when she says that oracles lie, before she relapses into the first rhythm. This simple structure occurs in many of the arias. I love the resolution of this passage when the chorus discovers the word 'trivium', at first thoughtfully and polyphonically considering what it might mean and then — as the penny drops — repeating it grimly over a repeated chord in the orchestra.

After this point I sense the theatre of the absurd in the underhand way in which the drama unfolds; it has been very cleverly compressed from the original, where there are more options, and here we are not allowed to feel there could be any other outcome. Here there is absolute clarity. Jocasta's 'Oracula mentiuntur' is one of the more conventionally operatic moments: we get the immediate impression that she is trying desperately to cover up the truth. She begins to guess the implications of the events. Oedipus finishes their duet with the line, 'Skiam' ('I will know!'). Jocasta already knew.

While the characters are not generally identified with certain sounds or distinct rhythms, the Messenger has a contra-bassoon, the Shepherd a high tenor 'Hughes Cuénod' voice (the effect is comically grotesque, since we would expect it to be rough and deep). The comic interruptions of the chorus when the Messenger enters push the action along. The chorus is as directly involved with the action as any Verdi chorus. But this device — and the score suggests a masked hieratic choral presence, with antecedents in

Greek drama — is a very practical solution to the problem of the operatic chorus. Stravinsky and Cocteau accept that it is a rather static body, and they have made an observation about its effect.

As the story unfolds, it becomes evident that the audience response is crucial to the way in which the piece is conceived: we are fed with morsels of information, so that we know a little more than Oedipus, and so that we think we know everything but we don't. Certainly the *St Matthew Passion* comes to mind; Bach's chorus has to be (vocally) very flexible, singing chorales, choruses and sometimes conversational interventions. *Oedipus* also has a moral subject, and the oratorio tradition is one of teaching and pointing out a clear message. With the decline of religion, indeed, opera has become one of the biggest communal experiences in our Society. Yet it is rather surprising that it should be Stravinsky and Cocteau who teach us the simple moral not to be too arrogant and not to think that we know best. *Oedipus* is certainly not a mystical piece; on the contrary it makes us use our brains, challenging us to put the facts together.

The tragic crisis comes when Jocasta's suicide is reported — in a terrifyingly jaunty football-crowd chorus: the marching rhythm and forced cheerfulness clash with the text. The chromatic tune is to banal that a mob might sing it on a street-corner. (A feature of *Oedipus* is that all the events are reported.) Here the effect is particularly frightening, because it is deliberately insensitive to the death, with alternating passages of 3/4 or 6/8. Piccolo and Eb clarinet give a mechanical colour to 'Atrocissimum' ('most terrible') and the chorus builds up to the cries of 'foedissimam beluam' ('a beast most vile'). In this stylised drama, the music rears up only to die away.

Oedipus Rex stands very much on its own. The quiet, forgiving ending is reminiscent of Ravel's *L'enfant et les sortilèges* but even within Stravinsky's own *oeuvre* it is unique. In this story, everything is the logical consequence of what has gone before. *The Rake* has coolness and the suggestion of parody. But I know no other work with such ruthless clarity and logic and intelligence.

Oedipus before the Sphinx in Giorgio Marini's production, La Fenice, 1989. (photo: Arici & Smith)

On an Oratorio

Jean Cocteau

Jocasta has just hanged herself. The plague is at its peak. Nobody is seen out abroad. Thebes has closed its shutters in sign of mourning. Oedipus remains alone. As he is blind, he cannot be seen (sic)...

At Colone, he related: 'I did this thing.' I remained right in the centre of the room. My eyes could not bear the revoltingly bright light of that chandelier.   *Popular Mystery*

Any serious work, whether poetry or music, theatre or cinema, requires a ceremonial, lengthy calculations, a structure in which the least architectural fault would put the pyramid out of balance. But whereas in an oriental play or in sports events, figures and architectural detail refer to a code which everybody knows, ours answer to rules which are proper to ourselves and are unfit to offer proof of excellence.

The work on *Oedipus Rex* was not simple. I could not kill ear by eye. I had to be violent, respecting the mythological monstrosity of it. Indeed, this myth reaches us with the same silence that the flying saucers do. Time and space send us it from some planet the morals of which disconcert. I upset Igor Stravinsky's oratorio neither by the play nor the dances. I was satisfied with seven tableaux, all very short, lasting as long as my text, on a stage looming over the orchestra. It would be inexact to say that I was inspired by the Japanese Noh drama, though I did recall the exemplary economy of gesture, all with allusive force, which that offers. I was amazed by the understanding of the craftsmen which made it feasible for me to make the masks. When there was a problem to solve, nothing strange astonished them. I may add that the wars of 1914 and 1940 have cut a gap which authorises the younger folk to be unconcerned about knowing whether what they are doing is new or not. On the other hand, we both did and saw too many things not to be compelled to try some new ones. For if we ourselves are no longer young, our works must be. *Oedipus Rex* dates from 1923. In 1952, it became a ceremonial piece to mark our reunion after so many years passed far from one another.   *Figaro Album,* June-July, 1952

*

It was only in Vienna, on the stage, beside a forest of instruments, facing the crowds in stalls, boxes, and galleries applauding Stravinsky across my presence, that I had the real feeling of the mime, which I had not been able to bring to Austria but which had been produced even at the Champs-Elysées theatre without my really seeing it at all. It all took place behind my back. I followed it in the audience's eye. At the Konzerthaus I actually saw it at last, all obstacles cleared, free from my own uncertainties, no longer obliged to wonder whether it was running properly. The impression was so powerful every time, urged on by the leader of the orchestra, and upborne by the waves of applause, that I forgot it was a pure concert version they were producing. In my imagination was an audience which had just seen the whole thing in its original form. This impression, I should make clear, was re-doubled since, never having actually seen the show myself, never having measured it except by the broad expanse of shadow or of light spread over the audience by the rise and fall of the curtain, I could believe that the mime and décor had always been invisible, that it was my inward tensions alone that even in the full stage production communicated it to the hall, quite as if I were a hypnotist. Thus Vienna actually did see it — by hypnosis — of that I was absolutely sure when I mounted the stage for the fifteenth time. Only the regrets expressed to me subsequently about the absence of the acting and all Vienna's demands for exact information regarding the real production, awakened me from that state of self hypnosis in which I found myself. So, to make it visible for them, I resolved to put in writing what in the Vienna concert hall I told our audience. But before even the mechanics of its mime, to me *Oedipus Rex* meant: Villefranche, Mont-Boron, Stravinsky and his family, my own youth, and all that of which I speak in the chapter entitled 'Birth of a Poem'. It was as if the period which separated that chapter from the one I am now writing were non-existent and I were relating both at the same time. No doubt that came from sensing the presence of Stravinsky on my left, as well as from the fact that memory substituted its own theatre for that in which I was merely the narrating voice.

*

The reason I am recording these memories as I did for my ballet *Le jeune homme et la mort* in *La difficulté d'être*, is that theatre shows evaporate, erode, crumble away. Of not one of the many plays which I have produced have I even photographs left. No, not even a bit of such flotsam of my *Roméo et Juliet* in the *Soirées de Paris*. That was the production in which together with Jean and Valentine Hugo, I invented the use of a black background, with only colours of the costume arabesques and any stage furniture visible. Red lights edging the outer frame of the stage prevented the audience distinguishing anything beyond that. Servants thus made invisible built up streets and interior walls about the choreographic movements of the performers. I formalised a very intriguing gait for the youth of Verona, Romeo alone not moving according to that exaggerated stylisation. But where indeed have last year's snows gone?

*

The masks in *Oedipus Rex* were fashioned for being seen from below. When viewed on a level they became illegible. They were mostly ovoid, the eyes set at the end of wands for horns. The hair was of raffia. Ridges of cork, wires, excrescences, isolated from the surface, indicated nose, ears, mouths. This was all surmounted by sheaves of corn which ended in red-painted ping-pong balls — what our French Midi would call *semble-sang*, 'mock-bleed'.

*

Gesture which never went as far as dancing, hardly exceeding pantomime, was essential for equilibrium between masks and orchestra. The mere raising of an arm or taking a forward step becomes of extreme importance with a masked figure. It is comparable with the violinist's arm itself suggesting the sound. The fact that the actor's arms are made miniature by the immensity of the mask makes them stand out, fourfold, not in volume, but in visibility. Beyond that, costume was not necessary. We merely had to suggest it on the background of black tights, ruling out artistic drapery. For hanging, I used rather heavy materials, so that the flow of them should not confuse the body's outlines. Otherwise, my actors would not have been actors with false heads, but dwarfs with enormous ones. I did not make the mistake of *Le boeuf sur le toit*, that error into which I dragged Dufy, but

22

which Picasso pointed out to me. Every one of my artificial heads was of a different size and architecture. The voluminous final mask of the blind Oedipus was amplified by the white globes of the heads of his daughters and the oval motif worked into the chorus costumes.

The work took a month of preparation, then a month of realisation by the craftsmen who helped me. Laverdet handled the curtain and finished off the masks. Villat looked after the shapes. Mme. Bebko and her son managed some of the more subtle masks, such as the heads of horses and jackals and the features of Athene's bevel-square and green crest. The rest was made with whatever came to my hand (nails, old press-photographers' discarded bulbs), and the prodigious skill of Laverdet's assistants, who even before one explained it to them grasped the incomprehensible. It is important to bear in mind that the acting all took place high up and far away from one; I had to get it not merely across the footlights, but also across the whole orchestra and a full choir. The only thing that troubled me was being obliged to stand back to the stage, hence unable to do more than shoot a glance at it. I kept myself informed by watching the audience, of which I had a marvellous view from the proscenium and which (except for the incurable stupidity of a few faces), was most impressive in its immobility.

'Athene's Grief': Théâtre des Champs-Elysées, 1952. (photo: Roger-Viollet)

Description of the Tableaux
1: The Arrival, One Night, of the Plague at Athens

One sees the plague as a giant, with enormous pale green microbe head. It crosses the stage left to right before three young Thebans represented by one man with arms extended, in each hand a mask. Extreme left, an enormous realistic moon sweeps a slow muslin shadow left to right, this making the young man in the centre drop his two masks and face the plague. He goes up to the plague, falls to his knees, greets it and from the crook of one of the long red-draped arms takes a death's head, with which he covers his own face. He then moves left, when, overcome with a shaking fit, he

'The Sphinx': Théâtre des Champs-Elysées, 1952. (photo: Roger-Viollet)

crouches on the ground, back arched, then stretches out, prostrate and motionless. Now a second young man, leaving the moon device, comes down the steps extreme left, mounts the steps extreme right, perceives the plague, bends down, takes a death's head from the crook of the plague's black-draped left arm, and masks himself. He begins to shudder, and the curtain falls.

2: Athene's Grief

The curtain rises, to reveal two pale blue frames on which, facing each other, like reflections, are painted line-drawings of Pallas Athene, formed from the figures 7, 4, 0 and 1 and the hook of a 3. These frames are held from the outside by two men with the heads and tails of black horses. A sky-blue drop-cloth bearing an eye on it lowers crests which crown the two bearers, leaving a little free space between the two frames and the bottom of the triangle. When the drop-cloth becomes still, Athene mounts a stair in the centre of the stage which leads to behind this sort of frame or temple, where it ends in a plinth. Her features consist of a green bevel square surmounted by a green-crested helmet. In her right hand she carries a lance, in the left a green buckler with cross-shaped relief simulating the Medusa's features. The shield is surrounded by writhing snakes. A double-ended spiral spring indicates the eyes.

Athene leans her forehead against a lance (profile right-left) her foot on another black plinth. Finally, she turns her head, so that we see it in left-to-right profile. After this, she comes to rest, facing the audience, raises her left arm and hides her face behind the shield, when her face becomes that of the Medusa and the curtain falls.

3: The Oracles

The curtain rises, to reveal three persons. In the centre, raised on an invisible cube, is Tiresias, in a yellow gown and black cloak. He has three

'The Oedipus Complex': Théâtre des Champs-Elysées, 1952. (photo: Roger-Viollet)

heads, one facing the audience, two in profile, these horizontal on his shoulders. On his left, back to the audience, is Oedipus, on his right, similarly back to the audience, Jocasta. Oedipus's head is egg-shaped. Jocasta's head is a pure ellipse. They both turn towards the audience. Tiresias's hands, black, are raised right and left of the central mask towards his throat. First Jocasta, then Oedipus too, pull at white ribbons, which as they move away from him, left and right, they draw out of the mouths of the two profile heads of Tiresias. When they reach the extreme right and left of the stage, the ribbons finally come out of the mouths of the shades. They gather them into their hands — Oedipus in his right, Jocasta in her left. They flourish them, then put them down, Oedipus against his heart, Jocasta against her belly. Then they let the ribbons fall to the ground, and spread wide their empty hands. Tiresias resumes his former posture and the curtain falls.

4: The Sphinx

The curtain rises on a long, low terracotta wall on which are painted black zigzag lines, with white relief. To right and left, at either end of the wall, is a man with jackal head. Near the left-hand jackal one sees the Sphinx, in profile, facing the right-hand jackal. The Sphinx moves backwards. It wears its head and shoulders mask hanging down on the shoulders of the actor. Its extended arms are hidden by white pointed wings. On its left flank is fastened a bird's tail, which one realises when it raises one knee. It opens its wings, which had been dangling loose, and raises them. They vibrate, and the actor bears them slowly, moving to the far right of the wall, which now completely hides his legs. Here the Sphinx halts, raises its left knee and shakes its wings. The curtain falls.

5: The Oedipus Complex

The curtain rises on a group of three actors in black tights. Two are on one

'Oedipus and his Daughters': Théâtre des Champs-Elysées, 1952. (photo: Roger-Viollet)

knee, the other leg stretched behind them. Their black silhouettes clear against a pale blue background, they have half-moon masks. Together, the two half-moons make a full moon. Behind, on a cube, is the third actor, in a mask which consists of the pupil of an eye centred in the white skeleton of a fish. This actor, arms crossed, conceals his body with a dark blue drapery. This he lets fall. At once, the half-moons separate and the actors who bear them move right and left. They about turn, to disclose a second profile silhouette. Returning to a position facing the audience, together with the central actor they make the gestures of drawing the figures 1, 3, 4 and 7 in the air. They are all three wearing white gloves. As the curtain falls the central figure ends up with the sign 0.

6: The Three Jocastas

The curtain rises on an empty stage, with — on the right of the centre steps — a dog formed by two actors, one standing with a jackal's head, the other bent, his arm round his partner's waist. A long black tail completes this silhouette. The third actor comes on by the central stairs, in his arms a doll representing the corpse of Jocasta (the mother). The actor sees the dog, falls back, turns round, tumbles down the stairs. Hanging, strangled by a red scarf, Jocasta (the wife) is lowered from the wings above. Her right hand is spread wide over her belly. Her foot projects below her robes. At once, the free actor reappears by the right-hand stairs, carrying a large head of Jocasta (the queen). The mouth of this head is open and from it emerges a long ribbon of red cloth. The dog begins to walk towards the left, followed by the actor carrying the head. Dog, actor and red ribbon form a procession which passes across stage under the hanging doll, and the curtain falls.

7: Oedipus and his Daughters

The curtain goes up to show two actors in black tights, at extreme right and left, on each slung a glazier's frame, from which dangle the masks of the

26

The back-drop: Théâtre des Champs-Elysées, 1952. (photo: Roger-Viollet)

choruses. By the centre stairs looms the voluminous mask of blind Oedipus. He comes forward till he is completely visible, then halts. His hands rest on the egg-shaped heads of his daughters. From each egg dangles a little frock, one pale mauve, the other pale blue. Oedipus kneels down and draws his daughters to his bosom. The choruses approach and take his daughters from him. They recede. Oedipus rises to his feet. With his left arm, he implores. The right-hand chorus comes back towards him and places one young daughter under his arm. Then Oedipus turns round and his daughter is passed from left to right hand. Now one only sees the back of Oedipus's black cloak and his hair, the red sheaves of his eyes and the egg with Antigone's pigtail. The group reaches the stairs and descends these as the curtain falls.

*

One might have feared that this final scene, so bizarre and aggressive, would produce laughter, but the audience seemed paralysed by a stupor of panic. We perhaps owed this climate of silence followed at last by a tumultuous ovation to the fact that in stylised presentation I had gone the whole hog, though of course the presence of Stravinsky conducting the orchestra added to the general jubilation. One can hardly be angry with the press men who saw nothing but grimace and caricature, when one recalls that even Charles Maurras says the primitive heads of the Acropolis museum are merely 'scarecrow things'.

The back drop was an enormous painted canvas (with greys, mauves, beiges and sulphurous yellow predominating) inspired by one of my drawings for *La Machine infernale*. Blind Oedipus and Jocasta, with distorted shapes, loomed from the rungs of this.

This chapter first appeared in Cocteau's 'Journal d'un inconnu' (1953), and this translation, by Alec Brown, in 'The Hand of a Stranger', 1956.

Thematic Guide

Many of the themes in *Oedipus Rex* have been mentioned in David Nice's article with numbers in square brackets. They tie in with these music examples and with the numbers in the opera text itself.

[1]

[2]

[3] OEDIPUS

[4a] CREON

[4b]

[5] OEDIPUS

[6] OEDIPUS

[7] TIRESIAS

Di — — ke - re non pos - sum,

[8] OEDIPUS

I — — nvi - di - a — for - tu - nam o - dit,

[9] TENORS, BASSES

Glo — ri - a, glo — ri - a, glo - ri - a!

[10] JOCASTA

Nonn' e - ru - be - ski - te in — ae - gra u - rbe cla - ma - re,

[11] JOCASTA

O - ra - cu - la, o - ra - cu - la, _____

[12]

JOCASTA O - ra — cu — la me - rti - u - (u) — ntur,

OEDIPUS Pa - ve — sco, ma - xi - me pa ve — — sco,

29

[13] MESSENGER

Re - ppe - re - ram in mon - te pu - e - rum

[14] SHEPHERD

O - por - te - - - bat ta - ke - re,

[15] OEDIPUS

Non - ne mon - strum re ski - tu - ri

[16] OEDIPUS

Lux fa - - cta e - - - st!

[17]

trumpets *f*

[18] TENORS

Mu - li - er in ves - ti - bu - lo, in ves -ti - bu - lo

Oedipus Rex

Opera-Oratorio in Two Acts
after Sophocles

by Igor Stravinsky

Text by Jean Cocteau
translated into Latin by Jean Daniélou

English translation of the Speaker's text by
e. e. cummings

English version of the Latin by Deryck Cooke

Oedipus Rex was first performed in concert, conducted by the composer, at the Théâtre Sarah-Bernhardt, Paris, on May 30, 1927. The first staged production was in Vienna (February 23, 1928), a few days before the production at the Kroll Oper, Berlin, conducted by Klemperer. There was a concert performance on February 24, 1928, in Boston, and the first staged production in North America was on April 21, 1931 in New York, conducted by Stokowski. The first performance in Britain was at the Queen's Hall, London, on February 12, 1936, in a concert conducted by Ansermet. Apart from performances by the Hamburg Opera at the 1956 Edinburgh Festival, the first British staged production was at Sadler's Wells on January 15, 1960, conducted by Colin Davis.

A note on the text

e.e. cummings' translation of the Speaker's text was commissioned by The Juilliard Opera Theatre.

Here we have adopted the usual English form of the name Oedipus for the English and English/Latin text but followed Cocteau and Daniélou in the French and French/Latin by spelling it with a capital dipthong, as it appears on the title page of the 1948 new revision of the score. This also gives a curious phonetic spelling in which 'c' was replaced by 'k' before certain vowels, but in this we have followed the libretto. In many places the Latin words are repeated in a different order from that in this text but the sense of Deryck Cooke's English translation is effectively complete. Nevertheless, to bring it rather more closely into line with the score, we have added a couple of lines where new words appear in these repeats, and adjusted the sequence of speeches to match what actually happens in the music. The score has also been the guide for placing the interventions of the Speaker, and for giving the few stage directions of a staging conceived for the first performance. This staging is described in detail, and illustrated with a sketch by Stravinsky's son, Théodore, overleaf, as well as Stravinsky's remarks about the misprints and obscurities of the Latin.

This décor presents the advantage of having no depth. It avoids the voices becoming lost. Everything takes place on one level.

The décor of the First Act is bathed in sunshine, in blue colour, decorated with white draperies. The Second Act has the same décor, except for a change of the background and the absence of the draperies. The new background is black. The Acropolis, which was lightly drawn in chalk on the background in the First Act, and which appears on the screen covering Creon, is again on the screen in the Second Act.

For the entry and exit of the characters, refer to the score. Except for Tiresias, the Shepherd and the Messenger, the characters remain in their built-up costumes and in their masks. Only their arms and heads move. They should give the impression of living statues.

The disappearance and reappearance of Oedipus in the Second Act takes place slowly, on the spot and by means of a trapdoor, as in a fairy scene. When Oedipus reappears, he wears a different mask, showing his misfortune; he is blind.

Jocasta remains on the balcony between columns. A screen (indicated by a dotted line on the plan) discloses or covers her. After her flight the niche remains empty, until in the same niche the Messenger is shown, who sings: 'Divum Jocastæ caput mortuum'. He carries a long trumpet with two tubes, which he puts to his mouth before he sings and during the fanfares, which interrupt the words of the Speaker.

Creon appears on the summit of the rocks. A screen (indicated by a dotted line on the plan) opens to discover him near his chariot and his horses, outlined on the canvas (as is the Acropolis). He remains until the end of the First Act.

Tiresias is the spirit of the truth, the spirit of the fount of truth. Complete night. Then the rocks below Creon are illuminated. They open and show a grotto. From this grotto Tiresias appears, a statue vaguely shown, concealed by veils flowing round it, which the projector has to follow up. After he has sung, Tiresias re-enters the grotto. The rocks close and light reappears. The Shepherd carries a young calf around his neck. The calf, the mask, and the costume form a shell which conceals the singer, and makes only his arms and legs visible. The Shepherd enters from the Left and sings at the foot of the steps, on the top of which Oedipus is placed. The same refers to the Messenger, who moves and delivers the end of his role from the balcony of Jocasta.

The chorus, in level front, is concealed behind a kind of bas-relief in three ascending tiers. This bas-relief represents a sculptured drapery, and reveals only the faces of the choristers.

The Speaker is in a black suit. He enters from the Left wing and comes up to the Proscenium. He leaves after he has spoken. He expresses himself like a conferencier, presenting the story with a detached voice.

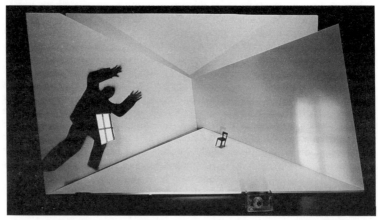

Set model by Nigel Lowery for David Alden's 1991 ENO production of 'Oedipus Rex'. (photo: Bill Rafferty)

Diagram for a staging by Théodore Stravinsky.

I used Latin rather than Greek, to answer your earlier question, because I had no notion of how to treat Greek musically (or Latin, Latinists will say, but there I did at least have *my* idea). I sometimes read in programme notes that the language of my *Oedipus* is 'medieval Latin', a rumour no doubt derived from the fact that the translator was a Catholic cleric. But the Latin, judging by the sentence structure, the placement of modifiers, and the use of the historical infinitive, is Ciceronian. I have found only one 'ecclesiastical' word in the whole libretto, and that — the *omniscius pastor* — can be called such only by association. (*Why* the shepherd should be omniscient I do not know.) Unusual grammatical constructions can be found — for example, the ablative form '*Laudibus Regina*' — which Daniélou may have borrowed from an old text — but they are rare. Idiomatically, the language is all pre-Boethian. But the Latinist is already horrified by the first letter of my score, the 'K', which does not exist in the language he knows. The purpose of this barbarian orthography was to secure hard, or at least non-Italianized, sounds instead of the usual potpourri of classic and ecclesiastic. I have misspelled a word, too, because of an error in transliteration from Russian: '*Miki*', at rehearsal number 50, is a mistake for '*Mihi*'.

'Stravinsky's scansion of the Latin syllables is sometimes rather unorthodox.' I quote a much quoted criticism. In fact, my scansion is entirely unorthodox. It must break every rule, if only because Latin is a language of fixed accents and I accentuate freely according to my musical dictates. Even the shift from '*OE*dipus' (which should be pronounced '*OY*dipus' by the singers and '*EE*dipus' by the speaker [The 'pus' must rhyme with moose, 'Tiresias' must be pronounced 'Tyreesias,' and Jocasta in three syllables — 'Iokaste'.] to 'Oe*DI*pus' is unthinkable from the point of view of speech, which, of course, is *not* my point of view.

I have noted in my own score that '*Vale*' should be '*Ave*' in the salute to Créon, as to say 'good-bye' at this point would be an incongruous intrusion of low comedy; that the grammar, and therefore the meaning [I no longer possess a copy of the French text, and I can only guess at the original meaning.] is obscure in the passage from '*Non reperias*' to '*istum pellere*', and that later in this same speech the construction '*Polliceor divinabo*' — 'I promise', or 'I shall guess' — is freakish; that '*accusat*' and '*accusas*' in the Oedipus-Tiresias exchange are misspelled; that the string of plosive consonants in Tiresias' '*Dicam, dicam quod dixit deus*' is good sound but bad Latin, though for this I claim musical licence; that the accent shift on the last syllable of each of the final '*Glorias*' — in the salute to the Queen — should be avoided by exaggerating the tonic accent; that 'Ment*iantur*,' in Iokaste's aria, is a printer's error, but a grave one: the Queen is supposed to say 'They lie — 'Ment*iuntur*' — not 'they may lie'; that '*Oedipoda*' is an unusual form and should perhaps be changed to '*Oedipodem*' or '*Oedipum*'.

Stravinsky, from 'A Greek Trilogy', 1968

CHARACTERS

Oedipus (Œdipe)	*tenor*
Jocasta (Jocaste)	*mezzo-soprano*
Creon* (Créon)	*bass-baritone*
Tiresias (Tirésias)	*bass*
The Shepherd (Le Berger)	*tenor*
The Messenger* (Le Messager)	*bass-baritone*
The Speaker	*speaking role*
Chorus	*tenors and basses*

*These roles may be sung by the same artist.

Michael Hordern as the Narrator, Sadler's Wells, 1960. (photo: David Sims)

34

Prologue

Ladies and Gentlemen,

You are about to hear a Latin version of King Oedipus.

This version is an opera-oratorio; based on the tragedy by Sophocles, but preserving only a certain monumental aspect of its various scenes. And so (wishing to spare your ears and your memories) I shall recall the story as we go along.

Oedipus, unknown to himself, contends with supernatural powers: those sleepless deities who are always watching us from a world beyond death. At the moment of his birth a snare was laid for him — and you will see the snare closing.

Now our drama begins:

Thebes is prostrate. After the Sphinx, a plague breaks out. The chorus implores Oedipus to save his city. Oedipus has vanquished the Sphinx: he promises.

Spectateurs,

Vous allez entendre une version latine d'Œdipe-Roi.

Afin de vous épargner tout effort d'oreilles et de mémoire et comme l'opéra-oratorio ne conserve des scènes qu'un certain aspect monumental, je vous rappellerai, au fur et à mesure, le drame de Sophocle.

Sans le savoir, Œdipe est aux prises avec les forces qui nous surveillent de l'autre côté de la mort. Elles lui tendent, depuis sa naissance, un piège que vous allez voir se fermer là.

Voici le drame:

Thèbes se démoralise. Après le Sphinx, la peste. Le chœur supplie Œdipe de sauver sa ville. Œdipe a vaincu le Sphinx: il promet.

Exit.

Stravinsky conducted the Santa Fe, 1960 production with Paul Franke (Oedipus) and Mary MacKenzie (Jocasta). (photo: Boosey & Hawkes, New York)

Act One

The curtain rises after the Prologue. On stage: Oedipus, the Chorus.

CHORUS

The plague is upon us,	[1] Caedit nos pestis,
Thebes is dying of the plague.	Theba peste moritur.
Save us, save us from the plague	E peste serva nos, serva,
Of which Thebes is dying.	E peste qua Theba moritur.
Oedipus, the plague is upon us,	[2] Œdipus, adest pestis,
Oedipus, save us from the plague,	Œdipus, e peste serva nos,
Deliver the city from the plague.	E peste libera urbem.

OEDIPUS

My children, I will deliver you,	[3] Liberi, vos liberabo,
I will deliver you from the plague.	Liberabo vos a peste.
I, the far-famed Oedipus,	Ego, clarissimus Œdipus,
I, Oedipus, love you,	Ego Œdipus vos diligo,
I, Oedipus, will deliver you.	Ego Œdipus vos servabo.

CHORUS

Save us once more, save our city,	Serva nos adhuc, serva urbem,
What is to be done, Oedipus, that we may be delivered?	Quid faciendum, Œdipus, ut liberemur?

OEDIPUS

The Queen's brother has been sent to consult the oracle,	Uxoris frater mittitur, oraculum consulit,
Creon has been sent to the God,	Deo mittitur Creo,
To ask what is to be done.	Quid faciendum consulit.
May Creon not be slow to return!	Creo ne commoretur.

CHORUS

Hail, Creon, we give you audience.	Vale, Creo! Audimus.
Hail, Creon, make haste!	Vale, Creo! Cito, cito!
Waiting to hear you, we salute you.	Audituri te salutant.

THE SPEAKER

Creon, the brother-in-law of Oedipus, has returned from Delphi, where he consulted the oracle. The oracle demands that Laius' murderer be punished. The assassin is hiding in Thebes; at whatever cost, he must be discovered. Oedipus boasts of his skill in dealing with the powers of darkness. He will discover and drive out the assassin.	Voici Créon, beau-frère d'Œdipe. Il revient de consulter l'oracle. L'oracle exige qu'on punisse le meurtre de Laïus. L'assassin se cache dans Thèbes; il faut le découvrir coûte que coûte. Œdipe se vante de son adresse à deviner les énigmes. Il découvrira et chassera l'assassin.

Exit Speaker.

CREON

The God gives answer:	[4] Respondit deus:
Avenge Laius, avenge the crime;	Laium ulcisci, scelus ulcisci;
Seek out the murderer.	Reperire peremptorem.
The murderer is hiding in Thebes.	Thebis peremptor latet.
The murderer of the king is in hiding; he must be discovered,	Latet peremptor regis; reperire opusistum,
To purge Thebes from the stain.	Thebas a labe luere.
Avenge the king's murder, the murdered king, Laius.	Cædem regis ulcisci, regis Laii perempti.

36

The God decrees: expel the murderer,	Jubet deus peremptorem depelli,
Who brought the plague on Thebes.	Peste inficit Thebas.
Apollo the God has spoken.	Apollo dixit deus.

OEDIPUS

You cannot right this ancient wrong; [5]	Non reperias vetus scelus;
I will have Thebes searched,	Thebas, Thebas eruam,
For the murderer is in Thebes.	Thebis incolit scelestus.

CHORUS

To you the God has spoken.	Deus dixit, tibi dixit.

OEDIPUS

To me he shall give himself up.	Mici, debet se dedere.
You must deliver him to me.	Opus vos istum deferre.
I solved the Sphinx's riddle, this one too [6]	Sphynga solvi carmen, ego divinabo,
will I solve.	
This further riddle will I solve, I, the	Iterum divinabo, clarissimus Œdipus,
far-famed Oedipus,	
Once more will I save Thebes.	Thebas iterum servabo.
I, I Oedipus will solve the riddle.	Ego, eg'Œdipus carmen divinabo.
I pledge my word to solve it.	Polliceor divinabo.

CHORUS

Solve the riddle, Oedipus, solve the riddle!	Solve! solve! solve! Solve, Œdipus solve!

THE SPEAKER

Oedipus questions that fountain of truth:	Œdipe interroge la fontaine de vérité:
Tiresias, the seer.	Tirésias, le devin.
Tiresias will not answer. He already	Tirésias évite de répondre. Il n'ignore plus
realises that Oedipus is a plaything of the	qu'Œdipe est joué par les dieux sans
heartless gods.	coeur.
This silence angers Oedipus, who accuses	Ce silence irrite Œdipe. Il accuse Créon
Creon of desiring the throne for himself,	de vouloir le trône et Tirésias d'être son
and Tiresias of being his accomplice.	complice.
Revolted by the injustice of this attitude,	Révolté par cette attitude injuste, Tirésias
Tiresias decides — the fountain speaks.	se décide. La fontaine parle. Voici l'oracle:
This is the oracle:	
The assassin of the king is a king.	L'assassin du roi est un roi.

Exit Speaker.

CHORUS

Delian goddess, we await thee, daughter	Delie exspectamus, Minerva filia Iovis;
of Jove;	
Diana, seated on thy throne;	Diana in trono insidens;
And thou, Phœbus, splendid archer, come	Et tu, Phæbe insignis iaculator, succurrite
to our aid.	nobis.
For evil swoops on us, swift in its flight,	Ut præceps ales ruit malum et premitur
death follows death, and in heaps lie the	funere funus et corporibus corpora
dead unburied.	inhumata.
Drive out and hurl into the sea this terrible	Expelle, expelle, everte in mare actrocem
foe, this Mars	istum Martem
Who comes unarmed, but shrieking madly	Qui nos urit inermis dementer ululans.
consumes us.	
And thou, Bacchus, come swiftly with thy	Et tu, Bacche, cum taeda advola nobis
torch, and burn up this god whom gods	urens infamem inter deos deum.
abhor.	

Hail, Tiresias! Hail! Tell us what the God decrees, tell us swiftly, O most learned in holy things.

Hail, Tiresias, thou great man, thou seer!

Salve, Tiresia! Salve! Dic nobis quod monet deus, dic cito, sacrorum docte.

Salve Tiresia, homo clare, vates!

TIRESIAS

I cannot speak, I may not speak,
It is not right for me to speak,
Oedipus, I cannot speak.
Do not force me to speak! beware lest I speak!
O far-famed Oedipus, it is best that I keep silence.

[7] Dicere non possum, dicere non licet,
Dicere nefastum
Œdipus, non possum.
Dicere ne cogas! Cave ne dicam!
Clarissime Œdipus, tacere fas.

OEDIPUS

Your silence accuses you;
You are the murderer.

Taciturnitas te accusat;
Tu peremptor.

TIRESIAS

Unhappy man, I will speak, since you accuse me.
I will reveal what the God has said, and keep back nothing;
The murderer is amongst you, the murderer is in your midst,
Is here with you. The slayer of the king is a king.
A king slew Laius, a king slew the king,
The God accuses a king; a king is the murderer!
He must be driven from Thebes.
A guilty king pollutes the city, a king is the murderer of the king.

Miserande, dico, quod me accusas, dico.
Dicam quod dixit deus; nullum dictum celabo;
Inter vos peremptor est, apud vos peremptor est,
Vobiscum est. Regis est rex peremptor.
Rex cecidit Laium, rex cecidit regem,
Deus regem accusat; peremptor, peremptor rex!
Opus Thebis pelli, Thebis pelli regem.
Rex scelestus urbem foedat, rex peremptor regis est.

OEDIPUS

Envy hates good fortune. Ye made me king.
I saved you from the Sphinx's riddle, and ye made me king.
Who should have solved the riddle?
Why thou, thou famous seer;
But it was I who solved it, and ye made me king.
Now there is one desires my office.
Creon desires to be king.
You are his accomplice, Tiresias! I see through your evil plan!
Creon desires to be king.
Who saved you from the riddle?
Friends, it was I, great Oedipus.
They desire that the King should die,
Great Oedipus, your King.

[8] Invidia fortunam odit. Creavistis me regem.
Servavi vos carminibus et creavistis me regem.
Solvendum carmen cui erat?
Tibi homo clare, vates;
A me solutum est et creavistis me regem.
Nunc vult quidam munus meum
Creo vult munus regis.
Stipendiarius es, Tiresia! Hoc facinus ego solvo!
Creo vult rex fieri.
Quis liberavit vos carminibus?
Amici, amici, ego Œdipus clarus.
Volunt regem perire,
Clarum Œdipodem, vestrum regem.

Enter Jocasta.

CHORUS

Glory, glory, glory!
Sing praises to Jocasta, Queen in stricken Thebes.
Sing praises to the wife of Oedipus. Glory!

[9] Gloria, gloria, gloria!
Laudibus regina Jocasta in pestilentibus Thebis.
Laudibus Œdipus uxor, Gloria!

Curtain.

Act Two

CHORUS
(*reprise*)

Glory, glory, glory!
Sing praises to Jocasta, Queen in stricken
 Thebes.
Sing praises to the wife of Oedipus.
 Glory!

[9] Gloria, gloria, gloria!
Laudibus regina Jocasta in pestilentibus
 Thebis.
Laudibus Œdipus uxor, Gloria!

Enter the Speaker.

THE SPEAKER

The dispute of the princes attracts Jocasta.

La dispute des princes attire Jocaste.

You will hear her calm them, shame them
for raising their voices in a stricken city.
She proves that oracles lie. For example,
an oracle predicted that Laïus would
perish by the hand of a son of hers;
whereas Laius was murdered by thieves,
at the crossing of three roads from Daulis
and Delphi.

Vous allez l'entendre les calmer, leur faire
honte de vociférer dans une ville malade.
Elle ne croit pas aux oracles. Elle prouve
que les oracles mentent. Par exemple on
avait prédit que Laïus mourrait par un fils
d'elle; or Laius a été assassiné par des
voleurs au carrefour des trois routes de
Daulie et de Delphes.

Three roads . . . crossroads — mark well
those words. They horrify Oedipus. He
remembers how, arriving from Corinth
before encountering the Sphinx, he killed
an old man where three roads meet. If
Laius of Thebes were that man — what
then? Oedipus cannot return to Corinth,
having been threatened by the oracle with
a double crime: killing his father and
marrying his mother.

Trivium! Carrefour! Retenez bien ce mot.
Il épouvante Œdipe. Il se souvient qu'
arrivant de Corinthe, avant sa rencontre
avec le sphinx, il a tué un vieillard au
carrefour des trois routes. Si c'est Laïus,
que devenir? Car il ne peut retourner à
Corinthe, l'oracle l'ayant menacé de tuer
son père et d'épouser sa mère.

He is afraid.

Il a peur.

Exit.

JOCASTA

Are ye not ashamed, O princes,
To raise your voices and fill a stricken city
 with domestic strife?
To shout your family quarrels,
To expose personal feuds in public?
Nothing is proved by the oracles, which
 always lie.
The oracles have lied.
Who was to have slain the King?
My son.
But the King was murdered.
Laius was murdered at the crossroads.
Nothing is proved by the oracles, which
 always lie.

[10] Nonne erubescite reges,
Clamare, ululare in ægra urbe domesticis
 altercationibus?
Clamare vestros domesticos clamores,
Coram omnibus clamare
Ne probentur oracula quæ semper
 mentiantur.
[11] Mentita sunt oracula.
Cui rex, interficiendus est?
Nato meo.
Age, rex peremptus est.
Laius in trivio mortuus.
Ne probentur oracula quæ semper
 mentiantur.

CHORUS

The crossroads! The crossroads!

Trivium, trivium, trivium!

OEDIPUS

Suddenly I am afraid, Jocasta,
I am afraid with a great fear.

Pavesco subito, Jocasta,
Pavesco, maxime pavesco.

39

Jocasta, Jocasta, did you speak of the crossroads?
I killed an old man, as I was coming from Corinth,
I killed him at the crossroads,
I killed an old man, Jocasta.

Jocasta, Jocasta, audi: locuta es de trivio?
Ego senem cecidi, cum Corintho excederem,
Cecidi in trivio,
Cecidi, Jocasta, senem.

JOCASTA

The oracles lie, always the oracles lie,

Oedipus, beware of the lying oracles
Let us go home at once;
Do not speak with the shepherd.

Oracula mentiuntur, semper oracula mentiuntur,
Œdipus, cave oracula quæ mentiuntur.
Domum cito redeamus;
Non est consulandum.

OEDIPUS

I am afraid with a great fear, Jocasta,
A great fear, Jocasta, is suddenly upon me.
I wish to speak with him, I must speak with him,
Jocasta, I wish to see the shepherd.
He is still living, the only witness of the crime. I must know the truth!

[12] Pavesco, maxime, subito, Jocasta.
Pavor magnus, Jocasta, in me inest.

Volo consulere, consulendem est,

Jocasta, volo videre pastorem.
Sceleris superest spectator. Sciam!

THE SPEAKER

The witness of the murder steps from the shadows. A messenger, announcing that King Polybus of Corinth is dead, reveals to Oedipus that he is only an adopted son of the king.

Le témoin du meurtre sort de l'ombre. Un messager annonce à Œdipe la mort de Polybe et lui révèle qu'il n'était que son fils adoptif.

Jocasta understands.

Jocaste comprend.

She tries to draw Oedipus back — in vain. She flees.

Elle tente de tirer Œdipe en arrière. Elle se sauve.

Oedipus supposes that she is ashamed of being the wife of an upstart.

Œdipe la croit honteuse d'être une femme de parvenu.

Oh, this lofty all-discerning Oedipus: he is in the snare. He alone does not know it.

Cet Œdipe, si fier de deviner tout! Il est dans le piège. Il est le seul à ne pas s'en apercevoir.

And then the truth strikes him.

La vérité le frappe sur la tête.

He falls. He falls headlong.

Il tombe. Il tombe de haut.

Exit. Enter the Shepherd and the Messenger.

CHORUS

The shepherd who knows all is here,
The shepherd who knows all, and a messenger with dread tidings.

Adest omniscius pastor,
Omniscius pastor et nuntius horribilis.

THE MESSENGER AND CHORUS

Dead is Polybus,
Dead is the aged Polybus.
Polybus was not Oedipus' father:
From me Polybus received him, I took him to the king.
Polybus was not the true father of Oedipus,
Only his adopted father, through me!

Mortuus est Polybus.
Senex mortuus Polybus.
Polybus non genitor Œdipodis:
A me ceperat Polybus, ego attuleram regi.

Verus non fuerat pater Œdipodis,

Falsus pater, per me!

I found Oedipus, a child abandoned on the mountains, [13]
Oedipus, a child with his feet pierced by shackles.
I brought the boy Oedipus to the shepherd.

Reppereram in monte puerum Œdipoda derelictum
Foratum pedes, vulneratum pedes parvulum Œdipoda.
Attuleram pastori puerum Œdipoda.

CHORUS

We are about to hear of a marvel, we shall hear of a marvel.
Oedipus was born of a great god; of a god and a nymph
Of the mountains on which he was found.

Resciturus sum monstrum, monstrum resciscam.
Deo claro Œdipus natus est; deo et nympha
Montium in quibus repertus est.

THE SHEPHERD

It would have been better to keep silence, never to speak. [14]
It is true that he found the child Oedipus
Abandoned by his parents on the mountain, shackled by the feet.
Would you had not spoken; this should ever have been concealed,
That Oedipus was found as a child, abandoned on the mountains.

Oportebat tacere, nunquam loqui.
Sane, repperit parvulum Œdipoda
A patre, a matre in monte derelictum, pedes laqueis foratum.
Utinam ne diceres; hoc semper celandum inventum
Esse in monte derelictum parvulum, parvum Œdipoda.

OEDIPUS

Are these not wondrous tidings you tell me, who Oedipus is? [15]
Let me know whose child I am.
Jocasta is ashamed, she flies from me,
She is ashamed of Oedipus the exile,
Ashamed of the descent of Oedipus.
Let me know who begot me, Oedipus the exile.
I, an exile, exult.

Nonne monstrum rescituri, quis Œdipus?
Genus Œdipodis sciam.
Pudet Jocastam, fugit,
Pudet, pudet Œdipi exulis,
Pudet Œdipodis generis.
Œdipodis genus, genus meum sciam, genus exulis mei.
Ego exul exsulto.

THE SHEPHERD, THE MESSENGER AND CHORUS

He was found on the mountains, abandoned by his mother;
We found him on the mountains.
He is the son of Laius and Jocasta!
The slayer of Laius his father!
The husband of Jocasta his mother!
Would you had never spoken, it were better never to have said this:
He was found on the mountains, abandoned by Jocasta.

In monte reppertus est, a matre derelictus;
In montibus repperimus.
Laio Jocastaque natus!
Peremptor Laii parentis!
Coniux Jocastæ parentis!
Utinam ne diceres, oportebat tacere nunquam dicere istud:
A Jocasta derelictum in monte reppertus est.

The Shepherd and the Messenger withdraw.

OEDIPUS

Sinful was my begetting, sinful my marriage,
Sinful my shedding of blood.
My light is put out! [16]

Natus sum quo nefastum est, concubui cui nefastum est,
Cecidi quem nefastum est.
Lux facta est!

Exit. The Messenger returns. [17]

41

And now you will hear that famous monologue 'The Divine Jocasta Is Dead', a monologue in which the messenger describes Jocasta's doom.

Et maintenant, vous allez entendre le monologue illustre 'La Tête Divine de Jocaste est Morte', monologue où le messager raconte la fin de Jocaste.

He can scarcely open his mouth. The chorus takes his part and helps him to tell how the Queen has hanged herself, and how Oedipus has pierced his eyeballs with her golden pin.

Il peut à peine ouvrir la bouche. Le chœur emprunte son rôle et l'aide à dire comment la reine s'est pendue et comment Œdipe s'est crevé les yeux avec son agrafe d'or.

Then comes the epilogue.

Ensuite, c'est l'épilogue.

The King is caught. He would show himself to all: as a filthy beast, an incestuous monster, a father killer, a fool.

Le roi est pris. Il veut se montrer à tous, montrer la bête immonde, l'inceste, le paricide, le fou.

His people drive him (gently, very gently) away.

On le chasse. On le chasse avec une extrème douceur.

Farewell, farewell, poor Oedipus! Farewell, Oedipus — we loved you.

Adieu, adieu, pauvre Œdipe! Adieu Œdipe; on t'aimait.

THE MESSENGER AND THE CHORUS

Jocasta the Queen is dead!
The woman in her chamber is tearing her hair.

Divum Jocastæ caput mortuum!
[18] Mulier in vestibulo comas lacerare.

They made fast the doors with bars, and lamented.
Oedipus broke in, beat on the doors,
Beat on the doors with cries of anguish.

Claustris occludere fores, exclamare.

Et Œdipus irrumpere et pulsare
Pulsare, ululare.

Jocasta the Queen is dead!
When Oedipus broke open the doors, they all beheld the Queen hanging there,
And Oedipus rushed to her, loosened the cord and took her down,
And snatching a golden pin from her dress, put out his eyes;
The dark blood ran down in streams.

Divum Jocastæ caput mortuum!
Et ubi evellit claustra, suspensam mulierem omnes conspexerunt
Et Œdipus præceps ruens illam exsolvebat, illam collocabat,
Et aurea fibula et avulsa fibula, oculos effodire;
Ater sanguis rigare.

Jocasta the Queen is dead!
The dark blood ran down in streams;
And Oedipus cried aloud and cursed himself.
To all he showed himself,
It was his will to show this horror.
See, the doors are opening,
Behold a sight of all sights most terrible.

Divum Jocastæ caput mortuum!
Sanguis ater rigabat, prosiliebat;
Et Œdipus exclamare et sese detestare.

Omnibus se ostendere
Beluam vult ostendere.
Aspicite fores pandere,
Aspicite spectaculum omnium atrocissimum.

THE MESSENGER

Jocasta the Queen is dead!

Divum Jocastæ caput mortuum!

Oedipus reappears. Exit the Messenger.

THE CHORUS

Lo! Oedipus the King: he shows himself to all as a foul monster, a thing most vile.

Ecce! Regem Œdipoda: fœdissimum monstrum monstrat, fœdissimam beluam.

42

Behold the blinded king! Wretched King
    Oedipus, slayer of his father,
Oedipus, the solver of riddles.
He is here! He is here! Behold him, King
    Oedipus!

Farewell, Oedipus! We loved thee well, we
    pity thee.
Unhappy Oedipus, we weep for thine eyes.
Farewell, unhappy Oedipus,
We loved thee well, Oedipus,
We bid thee farewell.

Ellum regem occæcatum! Rex parricida
    miser Œdipus
Œdipus carminum coniector.
Adest, adest! Ellum! Regem Œdipoda!

Vale Œdipus! Te amabam, te misereor.

Miser Œdipus, oculos tuos deploro.
Vale, miser Œdipus noster,
Te amabam, Œdipus,
Tibi valedico.

*Anne-Marie Owens (Jocasta) and John Treleavan (Oedipus), Scottish Opera, 1989,
designed and directed by Stefanos Lazaridis. (photo: Peter Devlin)*

William Hogarth, 'The Rake's Progress' engravings, 1735. (photos: Mary Evans Picture Library) 'The Heir.'

'The Levée.'

Making a Libretto: Three Collaborations over 'The Rake's Progress'

Roger Savage

Few flies on the wall can have had such an interesting time as the fly that was listening in on the conversations Stravinsky had with Wystan Auden in November 1947, assuming of course that flies were allowed into the Los Angeles home of the fastidious Stravinskys, which is where the conversations took place. Their topic was an opera Stravinsky wanted to write, to be based in some way on a picture-series which William Hogarth had first painted and then engraved in the 1730s, *The Rake's Progress*. Auden had agreed to be librettist; so, fuelled by coffee, whisky, nicotine and a trip one evening to a two-piano performance of *Così fan tutte*, composer and poet projected, planned and hypothesised together through the greater part of a week.

To that Angelino fly, Stravinsky and Auden must have presented a very odd spectacle indeed: the one Slavonic and 65, the other Nordic and 40; the one short and *chic*, the other tall, ungainly, unkempt; the one only partly at home in English, the other hyper-articulate in it; the one uxoriously straight, the other freewheelingly gay (freewheeling at least where sex, if not love, was concerned). To all appearances they were involved in a dialectic of creative opposites, the really odd thing being that they should be involved together at all. In fact, they had Stravinsky's great friend and Californian neighbour Aldous Huxley to thank that they were. The composer had for some time wanted to make an English-speaking opera as he now lived in the English-speaking world; and having pitched on a subject out of Hogarth, he had been on the look-out for a wordsmith; a purveyor of good English syllables and rhythms. Huxley recommended Auden, ostensibly because of his formidable talents as a versifier; and indeed, on the poet's arrival from New York that November, Stravinsky was properly impressed and delighted that Auden could extemporise specimens of *recherché* verse-forms — sestinas and the like — at great speed. This was something bound to appeal to a composer who, perhaps uniquely, had made the various things one can do with a verse unit, the French 'alexandrine', the basis for a movement in his ballet *Apollo* twenty years before.

But Huxley — Stravinsky later dubbed him the opera's godfather — probably had other things at the back of his mind which he knew would make the two seemingly polar types congenial to each other. For one thing, though their private lives would in different ways have shocked a narrow believer, both men were serious Christians. Then they were both deeply Euro-centred people who had nevertheless exiled themselves from Europe in 1939 and taken out American citizenship (the composer in '45, the poet in '46). And crucially both were 'makers'; that is to say, in the practice of their arts they saw themselves less as personal outpourers of inspired genius in a romantic-expressive tradition than as producers of sheer artefacts whose existence was in a vital sense independent of themselves as people. There was more than versification to unite them.

Before they had that first meeting in Los Angeles, Stravinsky and Auden had already exchanged a couple of tentative letters about the Hogarth project; and it was not to be until several weeks after their November conference that the plot of the opera was finally in place. Yet it was essentially during that week in Hollywood, 1260 North Wetherly Drive, that composer and poet got the

'The Orgy.'

'The Arrest.'

46

opera's working scenario up and running: a scenario which, they agreed, Auden would refine further when back in New York before turning it into the settable syllables of an actual libretto. In the early phase, however, it was not the poet who had the whip-hand. Stravinsky had for some while been thinking around the unusual notion of basing an opera not (as is most often the case) on a play or poetic myth or piece of prose fiction, but on a group of pictures: the Hogarth engravings which had caught his attention some months before at a show at the Chicago Art Institute. Clearly there was a fertile reaching-across-time from painter to composer. Auden, moreover, saw himself as the admiring junior partner in the project — 'I need hardly say that the chance of working with you is the greatest honour of my life' — and held that 'it is the librettist's job to satisfy the composer, not the other way round'; so it makes sense to ask what it was that had caught Stravinsky's eye about those eight Hogarths.

He said that he was struck by them 'as by a succession of operatic scenes', which is not surprising. The pictures imply a lively continuous drama, heated and histrionic enough to be sung. (At least one much earlier admirer back in the 1770s had been similarly struck and based a busy ballad-opera on them; this was submitted anonymously to Sheridan's Drury Lane Theatre but never staged.) The series charts the catastrophic 'progress' towards rakehood and worse of a young heir; and Stravinsky's opera as eventually written follows suit. It includes aspects, if no more than that, of all eight pictures, however much is changed and added (and a great deal is). To take the pictures one by one and to be very selective in describing them: in the first, our hero (or perhaps anti-hero) is seen as a callow young man coming into money and distancing himself from a former girl-friend. In the second he is surrounded by London's expensive sophistications and identified for us by a document included in the picture as 'T. Rakewell, Esq.'. In the third, we see him living it up rakishly in the company of some riotous and rather sinister low-lifers. In picture four there is an episode involving his sedan chair and a surprise meeting with his former girl. Next he becomes the incongruous groom of an unlikely bride while his girl languishes at a distance. In the sixth he is seen at a deadly game of chance, in the seventh as overwhelmed by debt and in the eighth as expiring in the madhouse, his girl at his side.

These are very partial accounts of the Hogarths; but the aspects which they do touch upon all figure in the opera (with their order symmetrically rearranged so that it runs 1, 3, 2, 4, 5, 7, 6, 8). It is clear that Hogarth's tentacles gripped Stravinsky quite tight, and there is an argument that this was for reasons beyond the dramatic vividness of his work. For one thing, the engravings are set in a very lived-in eighteenth century, and for nearly thirty years before that seminal Chicago visit much of Stravinsky's music had, in an idiosyncratic and creative way, been living in the eighteenth century too, using period resources (the pre-romantic becoming anti-romantic) in works like the *commedia dell'arte* ballet *Pulcinella*, the Octet and the Piano Sonata, the Duo Concertant and the 'Dumbarton Oaks' Concerto. For another thing, the pictures have an air of busily grotesque, even black, comedy: something which would have been appreciated by the composer of the fast and furious *Pulcinella* and the sharply satirical but splendidly energetic courtier-scenes in the miniature Hans Andersen opera *Le Rossignol*, to say nothing of the Russian grotesqueries in the one-act *Mavra* and the song-cycle *Pribaoutki*, with their tippling uncles, over-sexed hussars, shambolic colonels and gossipy wives obsessed by the servant problem. Again, the Hogarths imply an attitude to their story which is sternly moralistic in its treatment of the central character, yet with a hint of pathos at the close. (In the final picture the demented Rake,

'The Marriage.'

'The Gaming House.'

naked in Bedlam, is presented in a pose of near-monumental anguish which derives partly from the statue of Melancholy Madness which Caius Gabriel Cibber devised for the gateway of Bedlam Hospital and partly from the revered ancient marble generally known as the Dying Gladiator.) In the same way many male protagonists in Stravinsky's earlier theatre pieces are brought touchingly low by their own failings, whether fickleness, gullibility, lack of self-knowledge, blind optimism or complacent pride: the Emperor in *Le Rossignol*, Brer Rooster in *Renard*, the Soldier in *L'Histoire du soldat*, the fated Bridegroom in *Le Baiser de la fée* — and of course the King of Thebes in *Oedipus Rex.*

Add to this that Hogarth's tale reaches a vivid climax at a gaming table — Stravinsky had not only put prosody uniquely into ballet in *Apollo* but poker too in the 'ballet in three deals' *Jeu de cartes* — and the irresistible appeal of Hogarth for the composer becomes quite understandable. Their collaboration over two centuries seems almost a fated one. 'How I want thee, humorous Hogarth,' wrote Jonathan Swift in a satirical poem the year after the *Rake* engravings first appeared (and he pronounced the name to rhyme with the male lead in *Casablanca*); 'Thou, I hear, a pleasant rogue art . . .'. Stravinsky too wanted Hogarth, but he also wanted someone who could make drama of substance out of him; for, as it stands, Hogarth's sequence could not provide a plot strong enough for a full-length opera. The pictures have, if anything, too much bustling detail, while the story is too thin: a mere matter of the folly and come-uppance of T. Rakewell, Esq., the improvident big spender, however touching his final moments. Moreover, as Stravinsky the balletomane may have known, the composer Gavin Gordon and choreographer Ninette de Valois had in 1935 devised a ballet out of a fairly strict rendering into music and dance of six of Hogarth's eight tableaux. No point in doing that again: another humorous and pleasant rogue had to be brought in.

Enter Wystan Auden the librettist, late in 1947, fresh from writing some of his most brilliant and beguiling shorter poems ('Under Which Lyre', for instance, and 'The Fall of Rome') as well as the ambitious 'baroque eclogue', *The Age of Anxiety*. Could he bring the necessary enriching and sophisticating elements to the Hogarths? He had already been involved in the writing of five plays, to say nothing of texts for an operetta and an oratorio. But the Auden whom Stravinsky met was apparently an Auden in a serviceable and deferential mood, an Auden who seems, at first anyway, to have adopted the attitude of a skilled and solicitous midwife, tactfully and cannily drawing out and moulding the composer's own long-standing theatrical obsessions into a kind of *summa* of Stravinskian theatre. Certainly a lot of what was developed from Hogarth's pictorial material by the start of 1948 — not least the provision of an operatic villain — was foreshadowed in Stravinsky's earlier stage work: work which Auden seems to have known quite well.

Perhaps the crucial earlier piece is *L'Histoire du soldat*, the 1918 collaboration with the Swiss writer Charles-Ferdinand Ramuz. This is a highly sophisticated treatment of an archetypal folk story in which, *à la Faust*, a young Soldier allows his soul — in the form of his fiddle — to be bartered away by the Devil, who, wearing many disguises and having a remarkable control over time, provides various things in return: material comforts mainly, and a magic book which enables the boy to make a fortune, though this does not bring him much happiness. In what seems to be the tale's happy ending, the love of a good woman along with the interesting discovery that the Devil is an extremely rash gambler give the Soldier the courage and resourcefulness to beat Old Nick at a card game and so retrieve his soul (i.e., his fiddle). But the

'The Prison.'

'The Madhouse.'

real end is bleaker. The Soldier does not realise that his new-found happiness has limits and that if he tries to transcend them he will be damned. He does, and damned he summarily is.

A glance at the way Stravinsky and Auden expand on what Hogarth has to give them shows that they have let the ghosts of the Soldier and his Satanic friend happily haunt them (there was even a phase in early discussion when it was thought Tom Rakewell might have a violin). The new piece is, so to speak, 'Tom Rakewell's Tale'. In it the Father of Lies, disguised this time as the resourceful manservant Nick Shadow (a kind of sinister Jeeves to Tom's Bertie Wooster), cons his unwary, idle-minded master into a bargain. Old Nick, who has a remarkable way of making clocks stop or even run backwards, will serve him *gratis* for a year and a day, and only then claim his wages, which are unspecified but which will clearly be Tom's Faustian soul. In return, Tom will get all the things he dreams he wants: riches and pleasure (but they come to sicken him), happiness and freedom (but they prove illusory), and quasi-divine powers (but they turn out to be hollow and disastrous). Still, in what seems to be the tale's happy end, the inspiration of a good woman along with the lucky discovery that Nick is far too confident a card player conspire together so that, at the eleventh hour and 59th minute, Tom is able to retrieve his soul in a climactic game of cards. But the real end is bleaker. If the Devil, thwarted, cannot damn Tom outright, he can render his life a nightmare on earth by making him mad; and Tom dies in Bedlam when he finds the strain of a brief, blissful visit from his girl too great for his heart to bear.

In 1918 *L'Histoire du soldat* treated its folk motifs consciously as motifs: there is a knowing narrator and a flagrant mixing of idioms and media; it is all very proto-Brechtian. The scenario of the *Rake* thirty years later resembles *L'Histoire* in its self-conscious folksiness: the three wishes granted to the hero (for money, happiness and godlike power); the year-and-a-day formula; the clock that goes backwards; the nursery-book names of some of the characters (Mother Goose, Baba the Turk); the diabolic encounter in a graveyard at midnight; the cracker-barrel moralising. Then its eighteenth-century mask allows for much of the work's stylised, astringent distancing to be done through devices borrowed from the period's comedies of manners and *opera buffa*: the knowing asides to the pit, the principals delivering the epilogue in front of the curtain, the characterising names given to some characters (the Trulove family and the auctioneer Sellem, as well as Hogarth's original Rakewell). The mode in both pieces is 'once upon a time in a removed but relevant land of archetypes . . .'. (Hogarth the social commentator would have been amazed at what he had helped to sire!)

There is nothing exceptional about that 'once upon a time' in Stravinsky's theatre work. It is just as true of *L'Oiseau de feu*, *Le Rossignol* and *Le Baiser de la fée*, for all their differences in feel and musical idiom. And in other ways *L'Histoire du soldat* is not the only piece from which Auden could help the composer pick up things to strengthen their scenario and draw up good musical buckets from the Stravinskian well. For instance, the plot of *The Rake's Progress* could also be seen as a re-run — with a few changes — of the very Russian 'burlesque for singing and acting', *Renard*. There an idle and feckless Rooster falls for a series of flattering con-tricks played by a diabolical Fox and is saved in the nick of time by a friendly Cat and Goat. And individual scenes from the *Rake* libretto resonate with a whole range of Stravinsky works. A small example is the apparent death and startling resurrection of Tom Rakewell's ill-matched bride, the circus-artiste Baba the Turk, who sports, as Auden puts it, 'a magnificent Assyrian beard'. Baba herself is a splendid amalgam of an ambisextrous grotesquerie to rival that of the skirted but stubbly hussar-in-drag in *Mavra* with a noble artistic dedication to rival that of the godly protagonist of *Apollo*. But when she is 'buried' (under Tom's wig), only to be revived some months later while being sold off as a Mystery Object at the auction of the Rakewell estate, she takes us back to earlier miracles: to the apparently fatal stabbing of Pulcinella which is followed by an elaborate mock-magical resurrection, and to the cheerful cry of 'Greetings, all!' from the past-praying-for Emperor in *Le Rossignol*; even to the graduation to human-ghost-status of the puppet at the end of *Petrushka*. The idioms may differ, but the situation is constant.

Even more significant in this way is the scene of Tom's madness derived from Hogarth's last tableau, the first to engage Stravinsky and Auden together. When their hero is sent mad, he hallucinates that he is Adonis: golden youth, impetuous hunter and ruler of the Stygian Fields, where he spends his time awaiting the return of his mistress Venus, Queen of Love (alias Anne Trulove), and where his courtiers (alias his fellow Bedlamites) include Achilles, Helen of Troy, Persephone, Orpheus and Eurydice. On one level this invention works nicely as part of the period furniture of the libretto: the madfolk of Hogarth's original Bedlam suffer from delusions just as grotesque; and besides, comic-pathetic mad scenes in English drama and song around 1700 often involve decidedly unlikely people who think they are among the nymphs, swains, heroes and demigods of classical Greece. Thus the rakish Valentine in Congreve's *Love for Love*, pretending to be modishly mad, propositions Mrs Frail:

Harkee, I have a secret to tell you. Endymion and the Moon shall meet us on Mount Latmos and we'll be married in the dead of night. But say not a word! Hymen shall put his torch in a dark lantern that it may be secret, and Juno shall give her peacock poppy-water that it may fold its ogling tail . . .

But the deployment of such mythological charade-figures in the *Rake* also gives the opera a luminous gravity by taking Stravinsky's imagination back to the two ballets he had written around some of Tom's fantasy courtiers: *Perséphone* in 1934 and *Orpheus* in the year of the *Rake* scenario itself, 1947. So the last scene becomes, on one level, an exquisitely touching play-within-a-play sequel to the two ballets: a Masque of Venus and Adonis, of the Queen of Hearts and her mortal beloved who quests after a great beast only to have it turn and gore him. And it draws those ballets into itself when Anne/Venus, a second Persephone, brings spring to the wintry world of mad Tom and then, like a second Orpheus, charms and calms the wild hearts of the Bedlamites with a lullaby.

The libretto's creation of Anne Trulove is its final intensifier and enricher as a vehicle for Stravinsky's music, enabling a deep, persistent vein to be mined once more. It is not quite accurate to say that the libretto 'creates' Anne. Rather, she is *re*created from Sarah Young, the girl who appears in five of Hogarth's pictures. Sarah is a pathetic and clinging victim, promised marriage by our hero before he comes into money, made pregnant by him and bearing his child. The opera takes this soiled town lass and turns her into Tom's country sweetheart Anne, who responds virginally to what is best in Tom, loses him to his Shadow and the great beast which is London (the wild boar which forever threatens to kill Tom/Adonis), but follows him to the city and stays near him as a reminder of what might have been, bravely visiting him in the madhouse and giving him a timeless moment of fulfilment in the Venus-Adonis masque before she goes away to live *sempiterna virgo* with her father. Anne is a virgin-goddess who self-sacrificingly renews the dying year for suffering mankind. If Tom's ecstatic 'it is spring: the bridal couch is prepared' is one of the most moving moments in any opera, this is in part because the libretto has given Stravinsky an Anne who is a new emanation of the archetypical regenerative woman upon whom he had called several times before: as Persephone, as the Nightingale (a coloratura soprano) of the Hans Andersen opera, who returns to buy back the life of the Emperor, and as the sacrificial virgin of *Le Sacre du printemps*, dancing herself to death to ensure the renewal of her tribe. (As for the moment in the card game when Anne gives Tom the power to beat the Devil, it glances back to the moment in *L'Oiseau de feu* more than 35 years before, when the faithful Firebird puts her powers at the disposal of Prince Ivan so that he can destroy the infernal magician Kastchei.)

So what our fly on the wall would have heard in the study at 1260 North Wetherly Drive in 1947 was a self-effacing Auden, albeit a brilliantly resourceful one, helping Stravinsky to turn hints from Hogarth into a moral fable in eighteenth-century dress which would tap a considerable number of the composer's long-held obsessions and preoccupations. Hogarth's *Progress* is remade in Stravinsky's image. Yet in a collaboration which really chimed, and this one did — as Stravinsky said later, 'as soon as we began to work together, I discovered that we shared the same views not only about opera, but also on the nature of the Beautiful and the Good' — there was no reason why Auden should not remake the *Rake* story in his own image too, even before he began to invent the syllables the composer needed. Indeed, it could be argued that he would not have the creative engagement to produce half-decent syllables unless the project also tapped obsessions, preoccupations and attitudes of his own. And so he made sure it did.

The preoccupations of Auden the singular Christian — he had returned to the Anglican communion in 1940 after a twenty-year absence — are all over the libretto in its final form. (Not that Stravinsky would have jibbed at that; he had recently completed an austere setting of the Mass.) For instance, the quite unHogarthian locale of the first scene — the idyllic garden of the amiable Father Trulove — presents us with a Palladian Arcadia-cum-Eden, a rooted and fertile earthly paradise. But Paradise is about to be Lost. Eden-Arcady is invaded by Nick Shadow as the biblical serpent of temptation. (Later in the opera Baba will actually call him a snake.) Old Nick is able to try to seduce his victim into indulging the deadly sins of sloth, lust, gluttony and spiritual pride because the potential for them already lurks in a shadowy part of Tom's nature. Hence indeed the surname Nick is given: a name which suggests that in a sense Tom and Nick are the same person, and which links back to an earlier theatre piece of Auden's, the precocious and rum Morality written in 1929 with Christopher Isherwood and called *The Enemies of a Bishop*. There the hero has a dark double called The Spectre. The Spectre leads Robert, his human other half, through the valley of the shadow until Robert revolts:

ROBERT   You've cheated me all my life.
SPECTRE Really? I've done what you wanted me to.

Though Robert and Spectre were twinned under a 'twenties psychoanalytic star and Tom and Nick under a 'forties Christian one, both pairs are fine examples of the typically Audenesque 'double man'. (Auden would quote Montaigne on double men: 'We are, I know not how, double in ourselves, so that what we believe we disbelieve, and cannot rid ourselves of what we condemn.')

Nick the spectral tempter carries on the Christian, or rather inverted-Christian, theme with his response to each of Tom's folk-tale-type wishes. With the first ('I wish I had money'), whisking Tom off to the big bad city, Nick acts as his parody godfather in a mock-Anglican catechism-and-confirmation ritual which initiates the now-affluent Tom into the mysteries of metropolitan Venus. The ceremony is celebrated by a 'lady bishop' who is the Madame of a boisterous brothel and has Tom's virginity for fee. (It is much the same heady mix of St Augustine and *Playboy Magazine* that we find in Auden's astringent lyric 'The Love Feast', written in May 1948, two months after the *Rake* libretto was finished.) To satisfy Tom's second wish ('I wish I were happy'), Nick slyly inverts the Christian notion of marriage — affronting Auden's own preferred brand of Christian existentialism into the bargain — by convincing Tom that he should undertake an *acte gratuit* of the 'forties-fashionable *atheist*-existential variety. This entails lovelessly marrying Baba the circus freak and so rising 'freely' above both appetite and conscience. In answer to Tom's third, Utopian wish ('I wish it were true . . .'), Nick cons him into believing that he has invented a formula for turning stones into bread which will make him the ultimate Lord Bountiful, a god on earth. Tom has clearly forgotten his *Luke* Chap. iv, vv. 3-4, where making bread from stones is one of the Satanic temptations Christ rejects in the wilderness. ('The Devil bade me make stones my bread, / To have me break my true love's dance' are the words of the medieval carol 'Tomorrow shall be my dancing day'. Auden had long been fond of this text — could Anne's surname come from its obsessive repetitions of 'my true love'? — and in 1951 he introduced it to Stravinsky, who promptly set it in the *Cantata* of 1952, his first work after the *Rake*.) It is typical of this libretto that the 'fantastic baroque machine', as the stage direction puts it, for turning — or rather for not turning — bits of broken crockery into breakfast rolls should not only be parody-biblical but farcical too: even perhaps an allegory of the false perfectionism and dangerous machine-worship of the Industrial Revolution. It is much the same with the auction scene, when Tom's crazy flotation of shares in his world-saving machine has burst *à la* South Sea Bubble and his estate has to be sold off. The scene is not only a comic divertimento like the mock-auction in Henry Fielding's extravaganza *The Historical Register for the Year 1736*, but also a stylish evocation of the strange world of eighteenth-century collectors and *virtuosi*; into the bargain it is a satire on the degradation and misuse of the worlds of nature and high art when, in whatever century, their products are reduced to mere vendable commodities.

To return to Auden's Christening of *The Rake's Progress*; this does not end with Nick's perversions. It is turned right side up again by Anne Trulove, the blended embodiment of *eros, philia* and *agapë* (to use three favourite categories of the poet: romantic love, affectionate concern and Christian charity). It is Anne who knows that a love that is sworn before Heaven can plunder Hell of its prey. It is she who becomes a blend of indulgent mother, heavenly bride and priest-confessor in the Bedlam scene, and who in the end holds faith with Tom while commending him to a Higher Power: 'Tom, my vow holds ever, but it is no longer I you need.' *Sancta Anna*, one feels, *ora pro nobis*! And it is because Tom *has* prayed to her in his sad brothel-song as the wronged but constant goddess of love, and because he calls on her in a heroically absurd leap of faith *à la* Kierkegaard at the critical moment of his card game with Nick, that we have the feeling that he cannot be wholly damned.

Only a few years before, Auden had written *For the Time Being*, the libretto of a 'Christmas oratorio' meant for Benjamin Britten who in the end declined to set it because, as he said, it was 'too big and literary'. Auden's rather cryptic theology in the *Rake* meshes with that of *Time Being*. But the year before the oratorio he had also written a sonnet-sequence called *The Quest*, about an anonymous modern hero on an ambiguous and testing spiritual journey. Similarly, a kind of quest through a series of dream-landscapes which symbolise the human body for a while occupies the four acquaintances whose reflections on life, the universe and everything make up *The Age of Anxiety*, which appeared in the spring of the year Auden met Stravinsky; and in the same spring he was lecturing on quests at Barnard College in New York, telling his students to read *The Odyssey*, various Arthurian tales, *Faust, Don Giovanni, Alice in Wonderland* and so on. In fact he was quest mad, and he held it as incumbent on a questor to make sure he was not on a false quest. Significantly, the two most consequential plays he wrote in the mid-1930s with Isherwood — plays which he later called 'libretti *manqué*' — deal with quests which in different ways misfire. This makes them relevant to *The Rake's Progress*.

In *The Ascent of F6* a famous mountaineer goes in search of fulfilment for himself and glory for his nation by scaling a Himalayan peak. In *The Dog Beneath the Skin* a country lad, accompanied by a remarkably intelligent dog, travels far and wide through a European waste land in search of the missing squire of his village. But in *F6* all that the hero finds at the top of the mountain — in the playscript as first performed anyway — is a fatal confrontation with his own inner weakness and inadequacy; and in *Dogskin* the formal quest over Europe comes to nothing but the surprise revelation (once the questor is back in England) that the dog was the missing squire in disguise! Similarly with *The Rake's Progress*: Tom, as Adonis hunting the wild boar, quests after shadowy ideas of the good life by deserting the paradise garden and going from brothel to salon to loveless marriage to disastrous Stock Exchange speculation to anarchic bankruptcy; and all this only to discover that he has been on a false quest, and that what he should have sought has been near him with dog-like devotion all along. To borrow a recitative from the Advent section of *For the Time Being*:

> The garden is the only place there is, but you will not find it
> Until you have looked for it everywhere and found nowhere that is not a
>   desert . . .

Auden did not, however, bring only literary and spiritual preoccupations to the making of this 'mixture of fairy story and medieval morality play' (as he later described the *Rake* scenario). He brought a three-dimensional, physical preoccupation too, in the person of Chester Kallman, golden boy, gay Lothario and the unstill centre of Auden's life since 1939. Kallman had been Auden's lover, was still his close friend and would forever be his best-belovèd. To be psycho-biographical for a moment, there is a sense in which Kallman is actually part of the opera, as the hedonistic, idle, gullible yet buoyant, attractive and in-spite-of-everything-lovable Tom himself. And it is clear that Anne's selfless devotion for Tom is a reflection of Auden's love for his own 'shuttle-headed lad' (as Baba calls Tom), through thick and thin, reciprocity and wilful independence. (If one were to look, rather impertinently, for parallels in the composer's life, Tom would be little Igor himself, the bright boy unhealthily obsessed with money matters and other worldlinesses, while Anne would divide into his two wives: his childhood-sweetheart and first wife Catherine, about whom he came to feel increasingly guilty as his love turned elsewhere; and Vera, his second wife, who for 50 years — the two decades before their marriage in 1940 and the three after it — was, Persephone-like, his perpetually-renewing spring of fertility. Robert Craft, who was becoming an integral part of the Los Angeles household of Igor and Vera at the time of the composition of the *Rake*, has put it on record that the composer 'identified the love of Tom and Anne in their last scene with that of himself and his wife.')

Chester Kallman was not only loved by Auden; he was also his literary disciple, a writer of some promise; and in December 1947, soon after he returned from Los Angeles to New York with plans for the *Rake*, Auden involved Kallman in the project. The opera was generating a third collaboration: Hogarth-Stravinsky first, then Stravinsky-Auden, and now Auden-Kallman. Auden informed the composer of the arrangement rather brusquely: 'As you will see, I have taken a collaborator: an old friend of mine in whose talents I have the greatest confidence.' The phrase was not a diplomatic fudge on Auden's part: 'You are to me,' he had written intimately to Kallman on Christmas Day 1941, 'emotionally a mother, physically a father, and intellectually a son . . . I believe in your creative gift . . . I rely absolutely on your critical judgement.' Stravinsky, who had never met Kallman and may not have known of his existence, was rather ruffled at first. But he came to appreciate the 26-year-old New Yorker's contribution to the book (which was substantially finished by March 1948, only four months after that week of conversations at North Wetherly Drive). After all, in the mid-1940s Kallman was just as knowledgeable as Auden, indeed perhaps more knowledgeable, about the kind of 'number opera' of a Handel-to-middle-Verdi type Stravinsky was planning to take as the mould (his own word) in which to cast his piece. Kallman, Auden said, 'was the person who was responsible for arousing my interest in opera.' And he seems to have had a feeling for the role of words in large-scale musical structures which Auden had not yet fully grasped, for though there are 38 fine 'songs and other musical pieces' in Auden's *Collected Poetry* as issued in 1945, his two extended pre-Stravinsky texts for music do not work as well as libretti. *For the Time Being* is too wordy, while the operetta *Paul Bunyan* —which, unlike the oratorio, Britten had actually set — is not really strong enough in its central action. Kallman's valuable sensitivity in this area was presumably a reason for inviting his collaboration, quite apart from a loving concern to work with the younger man *and* to put him on the cultural map.

Together, Auden and Kallman devised some late-flowering aspects of the plot. For instance, young Tom originally called up the Devil by means of three yawns, which only now became three explicit wishes; the original diabolical machine was a sea-water-into-gold affair, which now became the stones-into-bread contraption; and there was originally an Ugly Duchess straight out of Hogarth's fifth tableau for the existential Tom to marry. *She* metamorphosed into a character much richer in potential and allegorical interest: the chattery, temperamental but golden-hearted artiste from St Giles' Fair, Baba the Bearded Turk. Baba is a strangely gifted, isolated man-woman who has to learn that her true talent is not for domesticity and mutuality but for the solitary perfecting of her art. Perhaps, among other things, she is a self-portrait of her librettists, especially the elder of them. (A camply melancholy Auden wrote to a friend six months before Baba was conceived: 'Miss God appears to have decided that I am to be a writer, but have no other fun, and no talent for making others as happy as I would like them to be.') Certainly the sympathy with which Baba is eventually treated prevents us thinking of the libretto as flat and formulaic, a rather puritanical matter of cardboard stereotypes. Puritanical, in the sense of being killjoy about human appetites, it is not. Auden as well as Kallman had his rakish side, enjoying a carnivalesque taste for wine, men and song; and the two librettists talked later of an instructive unwritten scene for the opera: an *intermezzo* in which those rather under-used characters Father Trulove and Mother Goose would bump into each other while Trulove was up in town on business, sing a rationally raunchy duet about the calls of the flesh and *exeunt* eagerly to the nearest convenient boudoir. The vice pilloried by *The Rake's Progress* is not physical license; it is idleness, very inclusively defined: that sleep of God-given energy which breeds monsters. Nick significantly and cruelly wishes Tom 'sweet dreams' near the start of the opera, and Tom confesses near the end that he has led his life 'in a foolish dream'. Those devil-summoning yawns in the draft-scenario had their point.

When it came to the actual labour of writing the syllables for Stravinsky to set, Auden and Kallman divided it pretty evenly, as well as criticising and modifying each other's work, so that on a verbal level it is quite unjust to think of the libretto as predominantly Auden's. Some of the book's most memorable phrases — memorable anyway when set to Stravinsky's music — are Kallman's: Tom's hollow evasion when Baba asks him who Anne is:

Only a milk-maid, pet,
To whom I was in debt,

or the *exalté* patter of Sellem's auction-waltz, or Nick Shadow's icy aside 'The Queen of Hearts again shall be for him the Queen of Hell' in the graveyard scene. Nevertheless, Kallman was understandably quite an Audenesque writer, and it is Auden's aesthetic which colours the whole text. The poet who wrote in a 1935 manifesto for the Group Theatre that proper dramatic characters (unlike characters in novels) should always be 'simplified; easily recognizable, and over-life size', and that 'the Music Hall, the Christmas Pantomime, and the country house charade are the most living drama of to-day', is here responsible for a libretto which unashamedly presents characters as archetypes and surrounds them with the devices of popular theatre, from the chorus line-up of molls and roarers in the brothel scene to Old Nick's descent through a trap door like a Victorian panto demon king. As for the language, its norm is urbane and poised in Auden's best public manner, though it is uncharacteristically economical and quite low on metaphor. (Britten's point about avoiding the 'big and literary' in texts for music had clearly been taken.) There are nice moments of jokiness and pathos, and a fine ease at moving into gently pastiched Augustan English when things need to sound like Alexander Pope's sonorous versions of the Greek and Latin classics, a scene from a Farquhar comedy, the trenchant lyrics of Gay's *Beggar's Opera* (which Hogarth himself had painted memorably) or the ones in the *Grub Street Opera* by Hogarth's admirer Fielding. The Augustan, however, is often Augustan-with-a-difference, flecked with the surreal; the Palladian architecture and Capability Brown landscapes look as if they have been redesigned by Giorgio de Chirico. Tom's sad reflections on his false questing are a case in point:

Always the quarry that I stalk
Fades or evades me, and I walk

An endless hall of chandeliers
In light that blinds, in light that sears,
Reflected from a million smiles
As empty as the country miles
Of silly wood and senseless park;
And only in my heart — the dark.

Make the Hogarthian world 'as contemporary as I treated Pergolesi in my *Pulcinella*', Stravinsky wrote to Auden; and Auden, with Kallman, complied.

The opera's set pieces call upon an impressively broad spectrum of verse-forms, metres and poetic idioms. The librettists 'vary the song', as Tom would say. An especially vivid strand grows out of Auden's advocacy in the 1930s for a serious interest in the forms and the merits of 'unofficial' poetry: popular songs, broadside ballads, nonsense verse, nursery rhymes, *vers de société*, Broadway lyrics and the like. His pioneering *Oxford Book of Light Verse* (1938) was the manifesto of this advocacy; and ten years later in the *Rake*, he is putting his creative talent where his enthusiasm is by composing fine pieces of serious light verse for the stages of Tom's quest. There is the wonderful nursery rhyme for grown-ups, 'Lanterloo, my lady', as Tom is initiated *chez* Mother Goose; some sinister, surreal, offstage nonsense songs for Tom and Nick when they have become anarchic social outcasts; and a perfect Tudorbethan fragment for Tom to sing when his wits are finally un-hinged:

With roses crowned, I sit on ground;
  Adonis is my name,
The only dear of Venus fair:
  Methinks it is no shame.

Such verbal inventions, along with a structure which is both lucid and intellectually respectable and a choice of dramatic situations calculated to touch the composer where he imaginatively lived, give the *Rake* libretto its strength. Its *made* quality, its expert and superintelligent artistry, meshes with the made quality of Stravinsky's score, its superb architecture of apt inventions. And both mesh with the subject, the need positively to construct a good life: 'to make the happiness one does not find', as Hogarth's younger contemporary Dr Johnson puts it in his *Vanity of Human Wishes*. (Have three!) In his diary of the years he spent *chez* Stravinsky, Robert Craft recalls a properly luminous and clinching remark of Auden's, uttered as he was moving somewhat vinously off to his room at the end of a lively hotel dinner with the Stravinskys in Berlin in the 1960s. 'After all,' he said, 'we were put on this earth to *make* things.'

The New and the Classical in 'The Rake's Progress'

Brian Trowell

'Neo-classicism?' he scoffed. 'A label that means nothing whatever. I will show you where to put it' — and he gave his derrière a firm pat.

Hubert Roussel was interviewing Stravinsky on January 25, 1949, for the *Houston Post.* The composer was known to be at work on a three-act opera with a libretto by W. H. Auden and Chester Kallman; and he apparently intended to confound modern expectations of what a musical drama ought to be by returning to the Mozartian conventions of a 'number' opera, with recitatives, arias and other set-pieces in closed forms. It would crown the thirty-odd years of his 'neoclassical' period, as critics and historians had come to call it. Roussel's line of questioning was therefore natural enough; but no one had warned him that Stravinsky detested the terms 'neoclassic', 'neoclassical', and above all 'neoclassicism', which seems to imply a movement or school with a shared credo and a uniform approach to musical composition.

On this last point Stravinsky was absolutely right, as modern critics are coming to agree, though they express themselves less picturesquely. Many composers in the 1920s grew tired of the emotional overstatement, formlessness, slow harmonic pulse, thick *legato* textures and orchestral gigantism of the late romantics, and started to base their music on the methods of the Viennese classics; but very important distinctions vanish if one lumps together as 'neoclassical' the essentially diatonic Stravinsky, the chromatic Hindemith and the panchromatic Schoenberg, to name only three (and besides, they also took models from pre-classical and early romantic music). Similarly in art: how much in common is there between Picasso's neoclassical drawings of the 1920s, Matisse's imitations of Ingres, and the Metaphysical paintings of de Chirico?

When asked 'What is theory in musical composition?', Stravinsky replied:

> Hindsight. It doesn't exist. There are compositions from which it is deduced. Or, if this isn't quite true, it has a by-product existence that is powerless to create or even to justify. Nevertheless, composition involves a deep intuition of theory.

The 'deep intuition of theory' must mean the sense of order, fitness, musical logic and proportion that results in a coherent style. A musical theorist may later seek to describe and codify such features and relate them consciously, as both composer and listener may have done unconsciously, to a whole repertory of experiences from earlier music; what the theorist says may be true, but that 'truth' will be secondary to, and will differ from, artistic 'truth'.

Faced with an aesthetic observation by Auden likening the temporal experience of music to that of living, Stravinsky offered a number of shrewd objections; but his first reaction was that 'this kind of thinking about music is a different vocation altogether for me: I cannot *do* anything with it as a truth, and my mind is a *doing* one'. So it was not simply that the theory of musical neoclassicism was half-baked — confusing in itself, and doubly so because it aroused all kinds of false expectations deriving from the theory and practice of eighteenth-century neoclassicism (the close imitation of Greco-Roman models): it was irrelevant to him simply because it was a theory.

This brings us to the third reason for Stravinsky's dismissal of the term 'neoclassicism'. It had been used as a stick to beat him with. Even his own adherents had found some difficulty in following him from the early ballets to *The Rite of Spring*, and many were severely upset by what he later called 'my aberrant "neoclassicism"'. The term itself achieved wide currency after the publication in 1928 of an article by, ironically enough, Stravinsky's friend and intellectual mentor Arthur Lourié, entitled 'Neogothic and Neoclassic'. He contrasted the 'neogothic' Schoenberg (whose disciples saw to it that the adjective did not catch on) with Stravinsky, associating the latter with the rationality, clarity, restraint, order and decorum of the true neoclassical ideals of the mid-eighteenth century. This article, though entirely positive, opened the way to dangerous confusion over Stravinsky's 'imitations'; for neoclassical theory had, since the Renaissance, advocated the closest possible imitation of the ancients, particularly in literary criticism, sculpture and architecture. The theory did not always sit comfortably on the creative artists of the time. Its principal musical exponent was Gluck, who actively set out to embody in his later operas the 'noble simplicity and calm grandeur' commended by the art historian Winckelmann; but Gluck worshipped Dionysus as well as Apollo and, having no antique music to imitate, created an entirely modern analogue.

There are certainly neoclassical qualities in Stravinsky's music, but his methods and aims in imitating the conventions, forms and other musical procedures of earlier music have almost nothing to do with eighteenth-century neoclassicism. That did not prevent his enemies from assailing each fresh 'neoclassical' work of his by saying that his 'imitations' betrayed not merely sterility but also incompetence. The attacks came from many directions. Teachers of academic harmony, counterpoint and composition, whose students were often required to write pastiche Bach or Mozart and who knew the routines of the (musical) 'classics' backwards, were simply baffled by the 'wrong notes'. Late romantic composers wishing to continue in the established paths, likewise. The other rival camp, the Schoenbergians, followed the master's lead (he actually took the trouble to enshrine a satirical squib on 'Modernski' in a musical canon). British opinion was strongly affected by Constant Lambert's attacks in *Music Ho!* (1934), with its accusations of 'time-travelling', surrealist grotesquerie and 'synthetic melody'. (Which melodies seem synthetic now, those of the *Symphony of Psalms* or those of *The Rio Grande*?) For a long time, Stravinsky's symphonies were not considered true symphonies, nor his concertos true concertos. The last prominent example of this kind of criticism dates from 1962, when Deryck Cooke complained that Stravinsky's Mozartian turns of phrase in *The Rake's Progress* did not develop in an authentic manner, as if Stravinsky were composing for the ear of the Emperor Joseph II.

Such attitudes, repeated in countless reviews, helped to delay the wider acceptance and performance of Stravinsky's works until recordings short-circuited the slow process of dissemination. But the misunderstandings that greeted his 'neoclassical' works must have astonished the composer as much as the furore over *The Rite of Spring*. He would have said of them, as he said of the much more violent *Rite*, 'I had only my ear to help me. I heard and I wrote what I heard'. Much later, in 1959 when he was writing serial music, he said:

> When I compose something, I cannot conceive that it should fail to be recognized for what it is, and understood. I use the language of music, and my statement in my grammar will be clear to the musician who has followed music up to where my contemporaries and I have brought it.

That puts the onus on the listener, and comes from a time when Stravinsky had money and a more assured position, when recordings, broadcasts, Arts Councils and the like had made it easier to address 'difficult' works to a specialist audience. In the 1920s he was less well-established, and one reason why many composers then turned back to 'old' music for their inspiration may have been that they wished to be more readily understood. That the 'old' music had refused to die was a new phenomenon in musical history; instead, it was perpetually present, crowding new works out of the concert schedules. If Stravinsky wished to make his music more approachable by adapting it to Western traditions as well as to reduced economic circumstances after the Great War, he would have been doubly mortified at the reception of his new style. Perhaps, like Bartók in his late works, he may have chosen to renounce the extremes of dissonance and complexity — and the vast and expensive orchestra he had hitherto been able to command — both in order not to get too far ahead of the intelligent public and in the hope of wider performance. In 1971, Auden quoted him as saying:

> What, may I ask, has become of the idea of universality — of a character of expression not necessarily popular but compelling to the highest imaginations of a decade or so beyond its time?

Moreover Stravinsky grew up in Russia, where he did not have the broad training in music and its history which he might have received in a conservatoire or a British university. When he settled in the West in 1910, there were great gaps in his knowledge of classical and pre-classical music; even when he heard performances of unfamiliar works, he may not always have been able to study them with a score (it comes as a surprise to learn that he did not possess scores of the Mozart/da Ponte operas when he first conceived *The Rake's Progress*, and had to ask his publisher Ralph Hawkes to send them to him). His 'neoclassical' compositions are in part the fruit of a process of discovery and self-education. His early works, as with any composer, were built on such discoveries, mainly of recent music and the folk music in his immediate environment: typically, when a piece of music, a sequence of notes, attracts a young composer, the composer learns it, studies it, imitates it and develops the elements which appeal, and, given a certain talent, a new and individual style is born. With Stravinsky, the investigation and assimilation moved back from Pergolesi into Renaissance and medieval music, onwards into the nineteenth century, and eventually to the serialism of Webern, from whom he evolved a style entirely his own. He recognized the same process in Glinka, and in a greater Westernised Slav, Pushkin, who, he said,

> was the most perfect representative of that wonderful line which began with Peter the Great and which, by a fortunate alloy, has united the most characteristically Russian elements with the spiritual riches of the West...
> As for myself, I had always been aware that I had in me the germs of

this same mentality only needing development, and I subsequently deliberately cultivated it.

Both of these are in prose, and were intended as recitatives, yet Stravinsky has organized them like arias. In his first instructions to Auden he suggested that he wanted no recitative at all: in other words, the work would have been something more like a ballad opera, no doubt with a minimum of speech. In his programme note, he said that 'The story is told, enacted, contained entirely in song'. Later he added further observations before this passage: 'In the earlier scenes the mould is to a certain extent pre-Gluck in that it tends to crowd the story into the *secco* recitatives, reserving the arias for the reflective poetry, but then, as the opera warms up, the story is told...'. It is interesting that he refers to Gluck and 'pre-Gluck', which almost certainly means the operas of Handel, because not many others were print in the late 1940s. One would have expected a reference to Mozart, since it was the da Ponte operas that he studied, borrowing dramatic motifs from *Don Giovanni* and musical inspiration from the other two, particularly *Così*. The immediate point, however, is that he at first found recitative an unwelcome idea, perhaps because he was not yet at home in English, more likely because he considered that it would lead to too many moments of broken tension and low-pressure music to which his style was not appropriate; there would have had to be different modern solutions to the old convention of joining the cadence of the recitative to the ensuing aria or other set-piece. And nothing in the *Rake* was to be routine.

Though he speaks of Gluck, no doubt the Gluck of *Alceste*, as a model for his continuous narration through song, he surely sneaked many a look at Verdi's last operas. Particularly in *Falstaff*, Verdi had found novel procedures to tell a story without recitative, and without resorting to Wagnerian methods. Gluck's responses were slower-moving and less varied, though there are echoes in the Bedlam scene. Of Verdi, Stravinsky said:

> The presentation of musical monologues seems to me more original in *Falstaff* than in *Otello*. Original also are the instrumentation, harmony, and part-writing, yet none of these has left any element of the sort that could create a school — so different is Verdi's originality from Wagner's.

Whatever the source of Stravinsky's solution to the problems posed by recitative, the results are masterly. The harpsichord (not used in the orchestral numbers) always strikes in appositely, because rarely: many passages marked for recitative in the libretto are set orchestrally and highly organized in melodic and motivic content. The 'prose' of the recitatives seems designed for this purpose, and often contains repeated and balanced constructions: 'I play the industrious apprentice in a copybook? I submit to the drudge's yoke? I slave through a lifetime?...' sings Tom. Mozartian and Gluckian recitative, of course, was not written in prose but in 'versi sciolti' of seven and eleven syllables, unrhymed except where a heightened tone was required: it is surprising how easily Auden's and Kallman's prose may be analysed into Italianate lines of three or five stresses.

Even where Stravinsky uses the harpsichord and a 'secco' style, he creates it anew, with unexpected progressions in the harmony, and looks for opportunities to organize the dialogue on musical lines. In the first scene of Act Two, where Nick presents Tom with Baba's picture, even the hackneyed dominant seventh becomes thematic and dramatically significant.

'Consider her picture', sings Nick on an A, against a 6/3 chord of B. Tom laughingly tries to escape into other keys, but Shadow keeps returning to his A, with the same harmony; Stravinsky interrupts the recitative by setting Nick's contemptuous philosophical monologue (still in prose) for strings in F major, but at its end Shadow returns to his original note and thematic colouring as the idea recurs: 'Consider her picture once more...'.

In this passage, Tom's replies are more sharply differentiated by string chords replacing and punctuating the harpsichord's. After the first scene of Act One, Stravinsky is liable to bring in another instrument or two while the harpsichord is playing, to reinforce vocal pitches, emphasize a bass-line, or add touches of colour and continuity. Eventually, after using less and less harpsichord recitative, he realises that the instrument's unique colour offers possibilities of its own, quite distinct from accompanying *secco* prose. After a long absence, it strikes into the terrors of the Graveyard scene, perfectly interrupting Nick's inexorable demands, as he casually suggests a game of card-guessing to torment his victim with false hope. The harpsichord music suggests the snap of the pack of cards, then the shuffling, and becomes figurative and thematic. The drop to a lower level of sound creates a desolate, deadly enclave where the least whisper is heard. It is barely disturbed — after some minutes — by a few, short, *pianissimo* woodwind phrases which increase the pathos of Tom's 'O God, what hopes have I'. But when he hears Anne's voice, as Shadow's unthinking words 'Love-lucky' and 'return' give him the clue to the correct answer, the simple entrance of the orchestral strings playing *forte* semiquavers, as he exultantly sings 'Love, first and last, assume eternal reign' (in a loose canon based on her first-act cabaletta), creates greater brilliance and resonance than Berlioz's four brass bands could have offered.

There is no space to discuss Stravinsky's use of the orchestra. Once again, the restrictions of Mozartian convention — strings, double woodwind, horns and trumpets, with timpani — lead to sharply-delineated, airy instrumentation, often decidedly unconventional, with *obbligati* and perfectly-spaced wind writing which produces a host of new sonorities, often near to chamber music. It sounds at its best in a small theatre. It was perhaps because he at first intended to include trombones that the writing for low-register trumpets is so extraordinary.

The small-scale use of harmony and distribution of notes within a chord, like the unusual resolution of chromatic leading-notes at the 'wrong' octave, suggest a man who listened to Mozart with very modern ears. If Mozart writes a triple appoggiatura at a cadence such as Example 1, Stravinsky will ignore the linear expectations and treat the dissonance as an invertible chord such as Example 2.

Ex. 1   Ex. 2

He often prefers to place his fifths at the top, not the bottom of the harmony, where they belong in classical practice. Or he will add an extra fifth beneath the tonic chord, as at the climax of the first chorus or with the bassoon drone in the 'Lanterloo' refrains (both in the second scene of Act One). He frequently substitutes a 6/3 where Mozart would have written a 5/3, as he does beneath Anne's first phrase or those of Tom's Bachian arias already mentioned; when combined with unexpected doublings (of major thirds, for instance), this can make for a certain fluidity, if not ambiguity, between a key and its mediant. He introduces into classical harmony the flattened sevenths and sharpened fourths of modal scales; but the richest source of chromatic harmony lies in the distancing of Mozartian grace-notes from the expected note of resolution. This may lead to a brilliant octave-displacement, with double-third appoggiaturas, as in the introduction to the Brothel scene (Example 3); or to a lugubrious accompaniment-figure (Example 4); and in both, as in Anne's first notes or in Example 5 from Tom's vocal line, one hears a mixture of minor and major, often because the appoggiatura is resolved at a different octave or in another part; it may be left entirely unresolved.

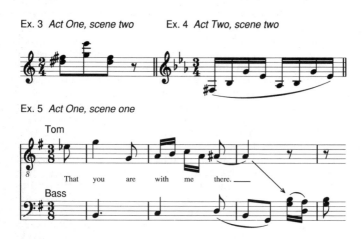

Ex. 3 *Act One, scene two*   Ex. 4 *Act Two, scene two*

Ex. 5 *Act One, scene one*

Tom

That you are with me there. ____

Bass

Most of these sounds are derived from Mozart's chromatically-decorated harmony, for example the accompaniment to Countess Almaviva's 'Porgi amor', but heard as vertical sonorities without the classical linear consequences. When the appoggiaturas are not resolved at all and placed in the bass, we seem to get two keys, though the ear apprehends the following passage, which accompanies Tom's dragging, fearful melody in the Graveyard scene, as G minor, with a modal D minor dominant (Example 6). The third bar of Example 6 suggests a mixture of G minor and F# major; transpose this down a semitone, rearrange the octaves and you have the sinister F# minor plus F major of the card-game later in the scene: here again the ear settles for F# minor, which the entry of Tom's tune will later confirm (Example 7).

Ex. 6

Ex. 7 *Duet*

Stravinsky's harmonic processes in *The Rake's Progress* have not received much attention from analysts, who have preferred his later and more systematic compositions: they have their own logic and compulsion, and the modulations clearly underline the words and the moods of those singing. Unlike Britten, he always knows how to move away and profit from the tension built up by holding the bass still. His usually admirable word-setting has been misunderstood. That strong beats may be displaced from barlines will not surprise listeners familiar with Tudor music or Dowland, or indeed Handel or Brahms. Stravinsky's sketches show that the disposition of the barlines was sometimes the last thing he arrived at: the music is conceived in terms of quantities rather than stresses. See how ingeniously and unexpectedly he contrives an unequal setting of the two equal verses of Tom's 'Vary the song' (Example 8). I have numbered each line to show how this formal repeat moves out of synchronization; later, a cut is made in the music. This principle of repeating music to new text in the modified strophic repeats favoured in the *Rake* is very unlike Mozart's way of repeating music in an aria where the text will be repeated as well.

Ex. 8 *Act Two, scene one: Tom's Aria*

Just as the words are never drowned, the conduct of the melody is clear, purposeful and always tuneful. If there are cross-references, as when important themes recur in the Graveyard scene, they are plain to hear. Some are unexpected, as when a fragment of the pastoral woodwind melody from the very first scene surfaces in the horn to haunt Tom's memory in Act Two, scene one, while he sings of his disgust with town life.

Ex. 9 *Act One, scene one*   Ex. 10 *Act Two, scene one*

Such processes may relate melodies in more subtle ways in widely-separated arias. Tom's Bachian offerings are both cast in the same mould, as may be seen by presenting them together with their pedal basses, and transposing the second into the key of the first.

Ex. 11 *Act One, scene two*

Ex. 12 *Act Three, scene three*

The Brothel song is far from the 'Serenade of the conventional gallant' called for in the original scenario, though that is just what the whores expect. It must have started life in the Graveyard scene, where the scenario says the 'Hero sings of lost innocence and love'; that is precisely what the Brothel song is about (and it calls on Love to save him, 'Lest I perish, /O be nigh/In my darkest hour'). The song must have been moved back partly because there it would have been too close to 'In a foolish dream' in the next scene but mainly because the scenario version of the Graveyard scene is childish and unsatisfactory. It was totally altered. (The scenario is printed, with an error or two, in Craft and Stravinsky's *Memories and Commentaries*, 1960, with the note that the 'outline... is not radically different from the published libretto'!)

There must have been further discussion by post or telephone, of which we know nothing. The idea of recasting the scene into a framing dialogue of ballad stanzas (by Auden), which frame the gambling scene with harpsichord and different verse-forms (by Kallman), offers a musical design so firm, relentless and ritualistic, that it must surely have been suggested by Stravinsky: it produces exactly the kind of structure that he loved, an alternation of short, sharply-contrasting, perfectly-proportioned movements carefully related in tempo. Is it significant that the Prelude (intended to begin Act Three, when the Auction scene was designed to end Act Two) was the first thing that he composed, before he had received a word of the final libretto?

67

The Prelude, for solo string quartet, is the darkness of the grave made palpable, particularly since it now follows the brilliant ending of the Auction scene. There is a rancid stench to the harmony when the full quartet plays from about the mid-point; no instrument rises above its D-string. The Prelude's thematic life has been thought mysterious, but seems clear if one listens to the moving parts. Example 13 gives it in aptly skeletal form. It begins with what seems to be a crawling worm in the solo cello, which recoils from the viola's D♭ (not shown) on the second beat of bar 2:

Ex. 13

Vcl. (a-string)

From the opening dip of a semitone, marked 'a', a four-note figure 'b' evolves; this is repeated and the line extends down, exploring each semitone until it settles on the open G-string. When the violins join in at bar 9, there is a wider version of 'a', now a full tone (a2), and an equally stretched version of 'b' (b3). At bar 13, 'b2' is unmistakably inverted three times in rising sequence, until the semitones of 'a' return insistently in the cello, to close on the dominant.

The coiling figure 'b' continues to play a part in the Graveyard scene. Tom's initial melody ornaments the progression D-C-E♭-D, and the viola, marked with a downbow, inverts it (see Example 6). The first two notes of the violins and viola present the figure as simultaneous harmony on the word 'dark' (D, then C+E♭+D); Stravinsky could have learned this device from undamped Russian folk-instruments, as well as from the serialists. Figure 'b' is also heard in the Bedlam scene, in the flute and oboe obbligato of 'In a foolish dream' (Example 14), and less clearly in Tom's melody and the revolving string accompaniment; also in Anne's line in the duettino with her father (Example 15).

Ex. 14   Ex. 15

Eve-ry   wear-ied   bo-dy   must...

The other thematic process unifying the Graveyard scene is a repeated musical end-rhyme, familiar enough in folk-music. Appropriately, it expands from a twice-repeated phrase in the folk-ballad (Example 16a). Since the ballad itself is so important in this scene, it can be no accident that both Tom and Shadow employ the same shape, stretched, for the ends of verses in ballad metre (Example 16b et seq.). At the moment of Tom's celestial madness, when 'Adonis' sings the ballad tune, we realize from the amazing ritornello for flute, oboe and clarinet (what an ear for harmonics and partials Stravinsky had!) that the ritornello, and therefore the similar music preceding Tom's entrance into the graveyard, also derive from the ballad tune, and indeed from its opening notes. The music also returns in the Bedlam scene in the duet with Anne, to accompany Tom's rapt transfiguration into Venus' true love. Taken together with the admirable analysis by Paul Griffiths (*Igor Stravinsky: The Rake's Progress*, 1982), we may see how powerfully these thematic devices complement the cohesive tonality and metrical proportioning of this extraordinary scene.

Ex. 16

La Scala, Milan took responsibility for the première at La Fenice, Venice in September 1951, seen here with Elisabeth Schwarzkopf (Anne), Otakar Kraus (Nick Shadow), Rafael Ariè (Trulove) and Robert Rounseville (Tom). The production was designed by Gianni Ratti (sets), Ebe Colciaghi (costumes) and conducted by the composer. (photo: Giacomelli/Boosey & Hawkes)

Tom finds no happiness in London. Act Two, scene one, La Fenice, 1951 with Robert Rounseville as Tom. (photo: Giacomelli/Boosey & Hawkes)

Thematic Guide

A few bars of each of the chief musical numbers in *The Rake's Progress* are given here, numbered in square brackets so as to tie in with the libretto.

[1] *Prelude*

[2] *Duet: Anne, Tom*

ANNE

The woods are green   and bird and beast at play

[3] *Aria*

TOM

Since it ____ is not by me - rit We rise or we fall,

[4]

NICK

Fair la - dy, ____ gra - cious gent-le - men,

[5] *Quartet: Tom, Anne, Trulove*

TOM

I wished but once, __ I knew That sure-ly my wish _ would come true, __

[6] *Duettino: Anne, Tom*

ANNE

Fare - well, fare - well, fare - well for now,

[7] *Terzettino*

TOM   (aside)

Laugh-ter and light, _____ and all charms that en - dear,

71

[8a] *Chorus*

ROARING BOYS

With air com-man-ding and wea-pon han-dy

[8b] *Chorus*

WHORES

In tri - umph glo-ri-ous with tro-phies cu-ri-ous

[9] *Cavatina*

TOM

Love, ____ too fre-quent-ly be - trayed ____

[10] *Chorus*

The sun is bright, the grass __ is green. Lan-ter - loo, __

[11] *Aria*

ANNE

Qui - - et - ly, night, ____

[12] *Cabaletta*

ANNE

I go, I go to him.

[13] *Aria*

TOM

Va - - - ry the song, __ O Lon-don, change!

72

[14] *Aria*

NICK

In youth the pan-ting slave pur-sues The fair e - va - sive dame;

[15] *Finale-Duet: Tom, Nick*

TOM

My tale shall be told Both ____ by young and by old, _____

[16] *Arioso*

ANNE

L'istesso tempo

No step, no step in fear ____ shall wan - der _____

[17] *Trio: Anne, Tom, Baba*

TOM

O bu - ry, o bu - ry the heart _____ there

[18] *Finale*

Poco più

[19] *Duet*

TOM

Thanks to this ex - cel - lent de - vice

[20] *Aria*

SELLEM

f

Who hears me, knows me; knows me A man with va - lue;

[21] *Duet: Anne, Baba*

BABA (to Anne)

You love him, seek _____ to set him right:

[22] *Stretto - Finale: Anne, Baba and Sellem with Chorus*

ANNE

I _____ go _____ to _____ him,

[23] *Duet: Tom, Nick*

TOM

How dark, how dark, _____ how dark and dread-ful _ is _ this place.

[24] *Duet: Tom, Nick*

TOM

My heart is wild with fear, _____ my throat is dry, _____

[25] *Chorus - Minuet*

Leave _ all love _ and hope _ be - hind!

[26] *Duet: Tom, Anne*

TOM

In a foo - - lish dream, in a gloo - my la-by-rinth _____

[27] *Lullaby: Anne and Chorus*

ANNE

Gent - ly, lit - tle boat, A - cross the o - cean float,

The Rake's Progress

Opera in Three Acts by Igor Stravinsky

A Fable by W. H. Auden and Chester Kallman

The first performance of *The Rake's Progress* was at the Teatro La Fenice, Venice, on September 11, 1951, in association with the Teatro alla Scala, Milan, during the Fourteenth International Festival of Contemporary Music at the Biennale, and was conducted by the composer. The British première was a BBC studio recording, broadcast on January 2, 1953: the first stage performance was by Glyndebourne Festival Opera at the Edinburgh Festival on August 25, 1953. The first performance in the United States was at the Metropolitan Opera, New York, on February 14, 1953.

The Orgy scene in the first London staging at Sadler's Wells, 1957. (photo: Hulton-Deutsch Collection)

75

Tom Rakewell   *tenor*
Nick Shadow   *baritone*
Trulove   *bass*
Sellem *an auctioneer*   *tenor*
The Keeper *of the madhouse*   *bass*
Anne *daughter to Trulove*   *soprano*
Baba the Turk   *mezzo-soprano*
Mother Goose   *mezzo-soprano*
Roaring Boys, Whores, Servants, Citizens, Madmen

The action takes place in an Eighteenth-Century England.

*Richard Lewis as Tom with Marko Rothmüller as Nick Shadow, Glyndebourne, 1954.
(photo: Guy Gravett)*

Act One

Prelude [1]

Scene One. *Garden of Trulove's home in the country. Afternoon in spring. House right, garden gate centre back, arbour left downstage, in which Anne and Rakewell are seated.*

[2] *Duet and Trio*

ANNE　　The woods are green, and bird and beast at play
　　　　　For all things keep this festival of May;
　　　　　With fragrant odours and with notes of cheer
　　　　　The pious earth observes the solemn year.

RAKEWELL　Now is the season when the Cyprian Queen
　　　　　With genial charm translates our mortal scene,
　　　　　When swains their nymphs in fervent arms enfold
　　　　　And with a kiss restore the Age of Gold.

Enter Trulove from the house and stands aside.

ANNE　　How sweet within the budding grove
　　　　　　To walk, to love.

RAKEWELL　How sweet beside the pliant stream
　　　　　　To lie, to dream.

TRULOVE　Oh may a father's prudent fears
　　　　　　Unfounded prove,

　　　　　And ready vows and loving looks
　　　　　　Be all they seem.

　　　　　In youth we fancy we are wise,
　　　　　　But time has shown,

　　　　　Alas, too often and too late,
　　　　　　We have not known

　　　　　The hearts of others or our own.

ANNE AND RAKEWELL
　　　　　Love tells no lies
　　　　　And in Love's eyes
　　　　　We see our future state,
　　　　　Ever happy, ever fair:
　　　　　Sorrow, hate,
　　　　　Disdain, despair,
　　　　　Rule not there
　　　　　But love alone
　　　　　Reigns o'er his own.

Recitative

TRULOVE (*coming forward*) Anne, my dear.

ANNE　　Yes, father.

TRULOVE　Your advice is needed in the kitchen.

Anne curtsies. Exit into the house.

TRULOVE　Tom, I have news for you. I have spoken on your behalf to a good friend in the City and he offers you a position in his counting house.

RAKEWELL　You are too generous, sir. You must not think me ungrateful if I do not immediately accept what you propose, but I have other prospects in view.

TRULOVE　Your reluctance to seek steady employment makes me uneasy.

RAKEWELL　Be assured your daughter shall not marry a poor man.

TRULOVE   So he be honest, she may take a poor husband if she choose, but I am resolved she shall never marry a lazy one.

Exit into the house.

RAKEWELL (*spoken*) The old fool.

Recitative   Here I stand, my constitution sound, my frame not ill-favoured, my wit ready, my heart light. *I* play the industrious apprentice in a copybook? *I* submit to the drudge's yoke? *I* slave through a lifetime to enrich others, and then be thrown away like a gnawed bone? Not *I*! Have not grave doctors assured us that good works are of no avail for Heaven predestines all? In my fashion, I may profess myself of their party and herewith entrust myself to Fortune.

Aria   Since it is not by merit
We rise or we fall,
But the favour of Fortune
That governs us all,
Why should I labour
For what in the end
She will give me for nothing
If she be my friend?
While if she be not, why,
The wealth I might gain
For a time by my toil would
At last be in vain.
Till I die, then, of fever,
Or by lightning am struck,
Let me live by my wits
And trust to my luck.
My life lies before me,
The world is so wide:
Come, wishes, be horses;
This beggar shall ride.

Rakewell walks about.

Spoken: I wish I had money.

Shadow appears immediately at the garden gate.

Recitative

SHADOW   Tom Rakewell?

RAKEWELL (*startled, turning around*) I —

SHADOW   I seek Tom Rakewell with a message. Is this his house?

RAKEWELL   No, not his house, but you have found him straying in his thoughts and footsteps. In short —

SHADOW   You are he?

RAKEWELL (*laughing*) Yes, surely. Tom Rakewell, at your service.

SHADOW   Well, well. (*He bows.*) Nick Shadow, sir, and at *your* service for, surely as you bear your name, I bear you a bright future. You recall an uncle, sir?

RAKEWELL   An uncle? My parents never mentioned one.

SHADOW   They quarrelled, I believe, sir. Yet he — Sir, have you friends?

RAKEWELL   More than a friend. The daughter of this house and ruler of my heart.

SHADOW (*He bows.*) A lover's fancy and a lovely thought. Then call her, call her. Indeed, let all who will, make their joy here of your glad tidings.

Rakewell rushes into the house, and Shadow reaches over the garden gate, unlatches it, enters the garden and walks forward. Rakewell re-enters from the house with Anne and Trulove.

SHADOW (*He bows.*) [4] Fair lady, gracious gentlemen, a servant begs your pardon for your time, but there is much to tell. Tom Rakewell had an uncle, one long parted from his native land. Him I served many years, served him in the many trades he served in turn; and all to his profit. Yes, profit was perpetually his. It was, indeed, his family, his friend, his hour of amusement — his life. But all his brilliant progeny of gold could not caress him when he lay dying. Sick for his home, sick for a memory of pleasure or of love, his thoughts were but of England. There, at least, he felt, his profit could be pleasure to an eager youth; for such, by counting years upon his fumbling fingers, he knew that you must be, good sir. Well, he is dead. And I am here with this commission: to tell Tom Rakewell that an unloved and forgotten uncle loved and remembered. You are a rich man.

Quartet [5]

RAKEWELL I wished but once, I knew
        That surely my wish would come true,
           That I
        Had but to speak at last
        And Fate would smile when Fortune cast
           The die.
        I knew. (*to Shadow*) Yet you, who bring
        The fateful end of questioning,
           Here by
        A new and grateful master's side,
        Be thanked, and as my Fortune and my guide,
           Remain, confirm, deny.

SHADOW (*bowing*)
        Be thanked, for masterless should I abide
        Too long, I soon would die.

ANNE (*reverently, as though startled from a trance*)
        Be thanked, O God, for him, and may a bride
        Soon to his vows reply.

TRULOVE Be thanked, O God, and curb in him all pride,
        That Anne may never sigh.

Rakewell puts one arm around Anne and gestures outward with the other.

RAKEWELL My Anne, behold, for doubt has fled our view,
        The skies are clear and every path is true.

ANNE   The joyous fount I see that brings increase
        To fields of promise and the groves of peace.

ANNE AND RAKEWELL
        O clement love!

TRULOVE   My children, may God bless you
        Even as a father.

SHADOW   Sir, may Nick address you
        A moment in your bliss? Even in carefree May
        A thriving fortune has its roots of care:
        Attorneys crouched like gardeners to pay,
        Bowers of paper only seals repair;
        We must be off to London.

RAKEWELL   They can wait!

TRULOVE No, Tom, your man is right, things must be done.
        The sooner that you settle your estate,
        The sooner you and Anne can be as one.

ANNE   Father is right, dear Tom.

SHADOW   A coach in wait
        Is down the road.

RAKEWELL   Well then, if Fortune sow
A crop that wax and pen must cultivate,
Let's fly to husbandry and make it grow.

Recitative

SHADOW   I'll call the coachman, sir.

TRULOVE (*to Shadow*)
                                    Should you not mind,
I'll tell you of his needs.

SHADOW   Sir, you are kind.

Exeunt Trulove and Shadow by the garden gate.

Duettino [6]

ANNE   Farewell for now, my heart
Is with you when you go,
However you may fare.

RAKEWELL   Wherever, when apart,
I may be, I shall know
That you are with me there.

Trulove and Shadow re-enter by the garden gate.

Recitative

SHADOW   All is ready, sir.

RAKEWELL   Tell me, good Shadow, since, born and bred in indigence, I am unacquainted with such matters, what wages you are accustomed to receive.

SHADOW   Let us not speak of that, master, till you know better what my services are worth. A year and a day hence, we will settle our account, and then, I promise you, you shall pay me no more and no less than what you yourself acknowledge to be just.

RAKEWELL   A fair offer. 'Tis agreed.

He turns to Trulove.

Arioso   Dear father Trulove, the very moment my affairs are settled, I shall send for you and my dearest Anne. And when she arrives, all London shall be at her feet, for all London shall be mine, and what is mine must of needs at least adore what I must with all my being worship.

Rakewell and Trulove shake hands affectionately. Anne brings her hand quickly to her eyes and turns her head away. Pause. Rakewell steps forward.

Terzettino [7]

RAKEWELL (*aside*)
       Laughter and light and all charms that endear,
              All that dazzles or dins,
       Wisdom and wit shall adorn the career
              Of him who can play, and who wins.

ANNE (*aside*)
       Hear, you are happy, yet why should a tear
              Dim our joyous designs?

TRULOVE (*aside*)
       Fortune so swift and so easy, I fear
              May only encourage his sins.

TRULOVE   Be well, be well advised.

ANNE   Be always near.

During the last lines, Anne, Rakewell and Trulove move toward the garden gate. Shadow holds it open for them and they pass through.

ANNE, RAKEWELL AND TRULOVE
Farewell.

SHADOW (*turning to the audience*)
The PROGRESS OF A RAKE begins.

Quick curtain.

Scene Two. *Mother Goose's brothel, London. At a table, downstage right, sit Rakewell, Shadow and Mother Goose drinking. Backstage left, a cuckoo clock. Whores, Roaring Boys.*

Chorus [8]

ROARING BOYS
With air commanding and weapon handy
We rove in a band through the streets at night,
Our only notion to make commotion
And find occasion to provoke a fight.

WHORES
In triumph glorious with trophies curious
We return victorious from Love's campaigns;
No troops more practised in Cupid's tactics
By feint and ambush the day to gain.

ROARING BOYS
For what is sweeter to human nature
Than to quarrel over nothing at all,
To hear the crashing of furniture smashing
Or heads being bashed in a tavern brawl?

WHORES
With darting glances and bold advances
We open fire upon young and old;
Surprised by rapture, their hearts are captured,
And into our laps they pour their gold.

TUTTI
A toast to our commanders then
From their Irregulars;
A toast, ladies and gentlemen:
To VENUS and to MARS!

Recitative and scene

SHADOW
Come Tom, I would fain have our hostess, good Mother Goose, learn how faithfully I have discharged my duties as a godfather in preparing you for the delights to which your newly-found state of manhood is about to call you.

So tell my Lady-Bishop of the game
What I did vow and promise in thy name.

RAKEWELL
'One aim in all things to pursue:
My duty to myself to do.'

SHADOW (*to Mother Goose*)
Is he not apt?

MOTHER GOOSE
And handsome, too.

SHADOW
What is thy duty to thyself?

RAKEWELL
'To shut my ears to prude and preacher
And follow Nature as my teacher.'

MOTHER GOOSE
What is the secret Nature knows?

RAKEWELL
'What Beauty is and where it grows.'

SHADOW
Canst thou define the Beautiful?

RAKEWELL   I can.
          'That source of pleasure to the eyes
          Youth owns, wit snatches, money buys,
          Envy affects to scorn, but lies:
          One fatal flaw it has. It dies.'

SHADOW   Exact, my scholar!

MOTHER GOOSE
                  What is Pleasure, then?

RAKEWELL 'The idol of all dreams, the same
          Whatever shape it wear or name;
          Whom flirts imagine as a hat,
          Old maids believe to be a cat.'

MOTHER GOOSE
        Bravo!

SHADOW   One final question. Love is . . .

RAKEWELL (*aside*)
                           Love!
          That precious word is like a fiery coal,
          It burns my lips, strikes terror to my soul.

SHADOW   No answer? Will my scholar fail me?

RAKEWELL (*violently*)
                          No,
          No more.

SHADOW   Well, well.

MOTHER GOOSE
                 More wine, love?

RAKEWELL   Let me go.

SHADOW   Are you afraid?

As the cuckoo clock coos ONE, Rakewell rises.

RAKEWELL   Before it is too late.

SHADOW   Wait.

Shadow makes a sign and the clock turns backward and coos TWELVE.

          See.
          Time is yours. The hours obey your pleasure.
          Fear not. Enjoy. You may repent at leisure.

Rakewell sits down again and drinks wildly.

Chorus

ROARING BOYS AND WHORES
          Soon dawn will glitter outside the shutter
          And small birds twitter, but what of that?
          So long as we're able and wine's on the table,
          Who cares what the troubling day is at?
          While food has flavour and limbs are shapely
          And hearts beat bravely to fiddle or drum
          Our proper employment is reckless enjoyment
          For too soon the noiseless night will come.

Recitative

SHADOW (*rising to address the company*) Sisters of Venus, Brothers of Mars, Fellow-worshippers in the Temple of Delight, it is my privilege to present to you a stranger to our rites who, following our custom, begs leave to sing you a song in earnest of his desire to be initiated. As you see, he is young; as you shall discover, he is rich. My master, and, if he will pardon the liberty, my friend, Mr Tom Rakewell.

Cavatina [9]

RAKEWELL (*coming forward*)

> Love, too frequently betrayed
> For some plausible desire
> Or the world's enchanted fire,
> Still thy traitor in his sleep
> Renews the vow he did not keep,
>   Weeping, weeping,
> He kneels before thy wounded shade.
> Love, my sorrow and my shame,
> Though thou daily be forgot,
> Goddess, oh forget me not.
> Lest I perish, oh be nigh
> In my darkest hour that I,
>   Dying, dying,
> May call upon thy sacred name.

Chorus

WHORES (*in turn*)

> How sad a song.
>   But sadness charms.
> How handsomely he cries.
> Come, drown your sorrows in these arms.
>   Forget it in these eyes.
> Upon these lips . . .

MOTHER GOOSE (*pushing them aside and taking Rakewell's hand*)
>   Away! Tonight
> I exercise my elder right
> And claim him for my prize.

The Chorus form a lane with the men on one side and the women on the other, as in a children's game. Mother Goose and Rakewell walk slowly between them to a door backstage. Shadow stands downstage watching. [10]

CHORUS
> The sun is bright, the grass is green:
>   Lanterloo, lanterloo.
> The King is courting his young Queen.
>   Lanterloo, my lady.

MEN
> They go a-walking. What do they see?

WOMEN
> An almanack in a walnut tree.
> They go a-riding. Whom do they meet?

MEN
> Three scarecrows and a pair of feet.
> What will she do when they sit at table?

WOMEN
> Eat as much as she is able.
> What will he do when they lie in bed?

CHORUS
> Lanterloo, lanterloo.

MEN
> Draw his sword and chop off her head.

CHORUS
> Lanterloo, my lady.

SHADOW (*raising his glass*)
> Sweet dreams, my master. Dreams may lie,
> But dream. For when you wake, you die.

> *Slow curtain.*

Scene Three. *Same as Scene One. Autumn night, full moon.* * *Anne enters from the house in travelling clothes.*

ANNE	No word from Tom. Has Love no voice, can Love not keep
Recitative	A Maytime vow in cities? Fades it as the rose
	Cut for a rich display? Forgot! But no, to weep
	Is not enough. He needs my help. Love hears, Love knows,
	Love answers him across the silent miles, and goes.

Aria [11]   Quietly, night, oh find him and caress,
            And may thou quiet find
      His heart, although it be unkind,
            Nor may its beat confess,
      Although I weep, it knows of loneliness.

      Guide me, O moon, chastely when I depart,
            And warmly be the same
      He watches without grief or shame;
            It cannot be thou art
      A colder moon upon a colder heart.

Trulove's voice is heard calling from the house — 'Anne, Anne.'

Recitative   My father! Can I desert him and his devotion for a love who has deserted me?

She starts walking back to the house. Then she stops suddenly.

            No, my father has strength of purpose, while Tom is weak, and needs the comfort of a helping hand.

She kneels.   O God, protect dear Tom, support my father, and strengthen my resolve.

She bows her head, then rises and comes forward with great decision.

Cabaletta   I go to him.
[12]   Love cannot falter,
            Cannot desert;
            Though it be shunned
            Or be forgotten,
            Though it be hurt,
            If love be love
            It will not alter.
            Oh should I see
            My love in need
            It shall not matter
            What he may be.

She turns and starts towards the garden gate.

                              Quick curtain.

---

1. The libretto has 'Summer night', but the score has 'Autumn night', and either Auden or Kallman corrected a printed copy in Texas to 'Autumn night'.

Act Two

Scene One. *The morning room of Rakewell's house in a London square. A bright morning sun pours in through the window; also noises from the street. Rakewell is seated at the breakfast table. Nearby, a wig-stand and wigs. At a particularly loud outburst of noise he rises, walks quickly to the window and slams it shut.*

RAKEWELL Vary the song, O London, change!
Aria [13] Disband your notes and let them range;
    Let rumour scream, let folly purr,
    Let Tone desert the flatterer.
    Let Harmony no more obey
    The strident choristers of prey;
    Yet all your music cannot fill
    The gap that in my heart — is still.

Recitative O Nature, green unnatural mother, how I have followed where you led. Is it for this I left the country? No ploughman is more a slave to sun, moon and season than a gentleman to the clock of Fashion. City! City! What Caesar could have imagined the curious viands I have tasted? They choke me. And let Oporto and Provence keep all their precious wines. I would as soon be dry and wrinkled as a raisin as ever taste another. Cards! Living Pictures! And, dear God, the matrons with their marriageable girls! Cover their charms a little, you well-bred bawds, or your goods will catch their death of the rheum long before they learn of the green sickness. The others, too, with their more candid charms. Pah!

Pause. Who's honest, chaste or kind? One, only one, and of her I dare not think.

He rises. Up, Nature, up, the hunt is on; thy pack is in full cry. They smell the blood upon the bracing air. On, on, on, through every street and mansion, for every candle in this capital of light attends thy appetising progress and burns in honour at thy shrine.

Aria (reprise) Always the quarry that I stalk
    Fades or evades me, and I walk
    An endless hall of chandeliers
    In light that blinds, in light that sears,
    Reflected from a million smiles
    All empty as the country miles
    Of silly wood and senseless park;
    And only in my heart — the dark.

He sits down. Pause.
Spoken: I wish I were happy.

Enter Shadow. He has a broadsheet in his hand.

Recitative

SHADOW Master, are you alone?

RAKEWELL And sick at heart. What is it?

SHADOW *(handing Rakewell the broadsheet)*
    Do you know this lady?

RAKEWELL Baba the Turk! I have not visited St Giles Fair as yet. They say that brave warriors who never flinched at the sound of musketry have swooned after a mere glimpse of her. Is such a thing possible in Nature?

SHADOW Two noted physicians have sworn that she is no impostor. Would you go see her?

RAKEWELL Nick, I know that manner of yours. You have some scheme afoot. Come, sir, out with it.

SHADOW Consider her picture.

RAKEWELL	Would you see me turned to stone?	
SHADOW	Do you desire her?	
RAKEWELL	Like the gout or the falling sickness.	
SHADOW	Are you obliged to her?	
RAKEWELL	Heaven forbid.	
SHADOW	Then marry her.	
RAKEWELL	Have you taken leave of your senses?	

SHADOW   I was never saner. Come, master, observe the host of mankind. How are they? Wretched. Why? Because they are not free. Why? Because the giddy multitude are driven by the unpredictable Must of their pleasures and the sober few are bound by the inflexible Ought of their duty, between which slaveries there is nothing to choose. Would you be happy? Then learn to act freely. Would you act freely? Then learn to ignore those twin tyrants of appetite and conscience. Therefore I counsel you, Master — take Baba the Turk to wife. Consider her picture once more, and as you do so reflect upon my words.

Aria [14]   In youth the panting slave pursues
        The fair evasive dame;
    Then, caught in colder fetters, woos
        Wealth, office or a name;

    Till, old, dishonoured, sick, downcast
        And failing in his wits,
    In Virtue's narrow cell at last
        The withered bondsman sits.

    That man alone his fate fulfils,
        For he alone is free
    Who chooses what to will, and wills
        His choice as destiny.

    No eye his future can foretell.
        No law his past explain
    Whom neither Passion may compel
        Nor Reason can restrain.

Pause.

SHADOW *(spoken)* Well?

Rakewell looks up from the broadsheet. He and Shadow look at each other. Pause. Then suddenly Rakewell begins to laugh. His laughter grows louder and louder. Shadow joins in. They shake hands. During the finale Shadow helps Rakewell get dressed to go out.

Duet-Finale [15]

RAKEWELL		SHADOW	
My tale shall be told.		Come, master, prepare	
Both by young and by old.		Your fate to dare,	
A favourite narration		Perfumed, well-dressed	
Throughout the nation		And looking your best,	
Remembered by all		A bachelor of fashion,	
In cottage and hall		Eyes hinting passion,	
With song and laughter		Your carriage young	
For ever after.		And upon your tongue	
For tongues will not tire		The gallant speeches	
Around the fire		That Cupid teaches	
Or sitting at meat		With Shadow to guide,	
The tale to repeat		Come, seek your bride,	
Of the wooing and wedding		Be up and doing,	
Likewise the bedding		Attend to your wooing,	
Of Baba the Turk		On Baba the Turk	

That masterwork
Whom Nature created
To be celebrated
For her features dire,
To Tom Rakewell Esquire.
My heart beats faster.
Come, Shadow.

Your charms to work.
What deed could be as great.
As with this gorgon to mate?
All the world shall admire
Tom Rakewell Esquire.
Come, Master
And do not falter.

RAKEWELL AND SHADOW (*together*)

> To Hymen's Altar.
> Ye Powers, inspire
> Tom Rakewell Esquire.

Exeunt.

Quick curtain.

Scene Two. *Street in front of Rakewell's house. London. Autumn. Dusk. The entrance, stage centre, is led up to by a flight of semi-circular steps. Servant's entrance left, tree right. Enter Anne. She looks anxiously at the entrance for a moment, walks slowly up the steps and hesitatingly lifts the knocker. Then she glances to the left and, seeing a servant beginning to come out of the servants' entrance, she hurries down to the right and flattens herself against the wall under the tree, her hand held against her breast, until he passes and goes off right. Then she steps forward.*

Recitative and arioso

ANNE   How strange! although the heart for love dare everything,
The hand draws back and finds
No spring of courage. London! Alone! seems all that it can say.
O heart, be stronger, that what this coward hand
Wishes beyond all bravery, the touch of his,
May bring its daring to a close, unneeded,
And love be all your bounty.

(with an elevated and quiet determination)
No step* in fear shall wander nor in weakness delay;
Hear thou or not, merciful Heaven, ease thou or not my way;
A love that is sworn before Thee can plunder Hell of its prey.

As she turns again towards the entrance, a noise from the right causes her to turn in that direction and come forward, as a procession of servants carrying wrapped, yet obviously strangely shaped, packages, starts crossing the stage from the right and exiting into the servants' entrance. While this is going on, night begins to fall. At its close the stage is dark.

What can this mean? . . . A ball? . . . A journey? . . . A dream?
How evil in the purple dark they seem . . .
Loot from dead fingers . . . Living mockery . . .
I tremble with no reason . . .

As the procession is completed, a sedan chair is carried in from the left, preceded by two servants carrying torches. Anne turns suddenly towards it. Surprised:

Lights! . . .

The chair is set down before the steps. Rakewell steps from it into the light.

Tis he!

Anne hurries to him, and he takes a few steps forward to meet her, and holds her gently away from himself.
Duet.

RAKEWELL (*confused and agitated*)
Anne! Here!

ANNE (*with self-control*)
And, Tom, such splendour.

---

* 'steps' in the libretto.

RAKEWELL Leave pretences,
Anne, ask me, accuse me —

ANNE (*interjecting*)
Tom, no —

RAKEWELL — Denounce me to the world, and go;
Return to your home, forget in your senses
What, senseless, you pursue.

ANNE (*quietly*)
Do you return?

RAKEWELL (*violently*)
I!

ANNE Then how shall I go?

RAKEWELL You must!
(*aside*) O wilful powers, pummel to dust
And drive into the void, one thought — return!

ANNE (*aside*) Assist me, Heaven, since love I must,
To calm his raging heart, his eyes that burn.

RAKEWELL (*turning to Anne and addressing her with a more measured tone*)
Listen to me, for I know London well!
   Here Virtue is a day coquette,
   For what night hides, it can forget,
And Virtue is, till gallants talk — and tell.
O Anne, that is the air we breathe; go home,
   'Tis wisdom here to be afraid.

ANNE How should I fear, who have your aid
And all my love for you beside, dear Tom?

RAKEWELL (*bitterly*)
My aid? London has done all that it can
   With me. Unworthy am I, less
   Than weak. Go back.

ANNE (*simply*)
Let worthiness,
So you still love, reside in that.

RAKEWELL (*touched, stepping towards her with emotion*)
O Anne!

Baba suddenly puts her head out through the curtains of the sedan-chair window. She is very elaborately coiffed, and her face is, below the eyes, heavily veiled in the Eastern fashion.

Recitative

BABA (*interrupting with vexation*) My love, am I to remain in here forever? You know that
I am *not* in the habit of stepping from my sedan unaided. Nor shall I wait,
unmoved, much longer. Finish, if you please, whatever business is
detaining you with this person.
She withdraws her head.

ANNE (*surprised*) Tom, what —?

RAKEWELL My wife, Anne.

ANNE Your wife!
Pause. Then, with slight bitterness
I see, then, it is I who was unworthy.

She turns away. Rakewell again steps towards her, then checks himself.

Trio

ANNE (*aside*)   Could it then have been known
When love was spring, and love took all our ken,
That I and I alone
Upon that forsworn ground,
Should see love dead?
Oh promise the heart to winter, swear it bound
To nothing live, and you shall wed;
But should you vow to love, Oh then
See that you shall not feel again —
Oh never, never, never —
Lest you, alone, your promise keep,
Walk the long aisle, and walking weep
Forever.

TOM (*aside*)   It is done, it is done.
I turn away, yet should I turn again,
The arbour would be gone
And on the frozen ground,
The birds lie dead.
[17]   Oh bury the heart there deeper than it sound,
Upon its only bridal bed;
And should it, dreaming love, ask — When
Shall I awaken once again?
Say — Never, never, never;
We shall this wint'ry promise keep —
Obey thy exile, honour sleep
Forever.

BABA (*poking her head out of the curtains at each remark*)
Why this delay? Away!
Oh, who is it, pray,
He prefers to his Baba on their wedding day?

A family friend? An ancient flame?
I'm quite perplexed
And more, I confess, than a little vexed.

Enough is enough!
Baba is not used
To be so abused.
She is not amused
Come here, my love.
I hate waiting,
I'm suffocating,
Heavens above!
Will you permit me to sit in this conveyance forever?

Exit Anne right hurriedly.

Finale [18] I have not run away, dear heart. Baba is still waiting patiently for her gallant.

RAKEWELL (*squaring his shoulders and approaching the chair*)
I am with you, dear wife.

He helps her from the chair with a gallant bow.

BABA (*patting him affectionately on the cheek*)
Who was that girl, my life?

RAKEWELL (*ironically*)
Only a milk-maid pet,
To whom I was in debt.

As Rakewell takes his wife's hand and lifts it to begin conducting her up the steps, the entrance doors are thrown open, Servants carry off the sedan chair. Servants appear from the entrance and line the steps, carrying torches, and voices are heard off, crying:

VOICES   Baba the Turk is here! Baba the Turk is here!

At this, Baba, as she begins her ascent, draws herself up with obvious pride — and the Crowd pours on to the stage from both sides.

CROWD (*facing the house — covering the whole front of the stage — in the darkness*)
          Baba the Turk, Baba the Turk, before you retire,
          Show thyself once, oh grant us our desire.
Baba and Rakewell have reached the top of the steps. He goes into the house, and she, with an eloquent gesture, sweeps around to face the crowd, removes her veil and reveals a full and flowing black beard. The Crowd, entranced, chants:
          Ah! Baba, Baba, Baba. Ah!

She blows them a kiss and keeps her arms outstretched with the practised manner of a great artiste. Tableau.

Curtain.

Scene Three. *The same room as Act Two, scene one. Except that now it is cluttered up with every conceivable kind of object: stuffed animals and birds, cases of minerals, china, glass, etc.. Rakewell and Baba are sitting at breakfast, the former sulking, the latter breathlessly chattering.*

Aria

BABA   As I was saying both brothers wore moustaches,
             But Sir John was taller; they gave me the musical glasses.
             That was in Vienna, no, it must have been Milan
             Because of the donkeys. Vienna was the Chinese fan
             — or was it the bottle of water from the River Jordan?
             I'm certain at least it was Vienna and Lord Gordon.
             I get so confused about all my travels.
             The snuff boxes came from Paris, and the fulminous gravels
             From a cardinal who admired me vastly in Rome.
             You're not eating, my love. Count Moldau gave me the gnome,
             And Prince Obolowsky the little statues of the Twelve Apostles,
             Which I like best of all my treasures except my fossils.
             Which reminds me I must tell Bridget never to touch the mummies.
             I'll dust them myself. She can do the wax-work dummies.
             Of course, I like my birds, too, especially my Great Auk;
             But the moths will get in them. My love, what's the matter, why don't you
               talk?
Pause.   What's the matter?

RAKEWELL   Nothing.

BABA   Speak to me!

RAKEWELL   Why?

Baba rises and puts her arm lovingly round Rakewell's neck.

Baba's song

BABA   Come, sweet, come.
             Why so glum?
             Smile at Baba who
             Loving smiles at you.
             Do not frown,
             Husband dear . . . .

RAKEWELL (*pushing her violently away*)
Spoken: Sit down.

Baba bursts into tears and rage. During the following she strides about the stage and, at each of the four words in the first lines of both stanzas, picks up some object and smashes it.

Aria

BABA   Scorned! Abused! Neglected! Baited!
       Wretched me!
       Why is this?
       I can see.
       I know who is
       Your bliss, your love, your life,
       While I, your loving wife —
       Lie not! — am hated.

       Young, demure, delightful, clever,
         Is she not?
         Not as I.
(shoving her face into Rakewell's)
         That is what
         I know you sigh.
         Then sigh! Then cry! For she,
She sits down.
       Your wife shall never be —
       Oh no! no, ne . . . (ver)

In the middle of the last word Rakewell rises suddenly, seizes the wig and plumps it down over her head, back to front, cutting her off suddenly. Baba remains silent and motionless in her place for the rest of the scene. Rakewell walks moodily about with his hands in his pockets, then flings himself down on a sofa backstage.

Recitative

RAKEWELL My heart is cold, I cannot weep;
       One remedy is left me — sleep.
He sleeps. A short pause.

Pantomime. A door right, opens and Shadow peeps in. Seeing all clear, he withdraws his head and then enters, wheeling in front of him some large object covered by a dust sheet. When he has brought it to the front centre of stage he removes the dust sheet and discloses a fantastic baroque machine. He looks about, picks a loaf of bread from the table; opens a door in the front of the machine, puts in the loaf and closes the door. Then he looks round again and picks off the floor a piece of broken vase. This he drops into a hopper on the machine. He turns a wheel and the loaf of bread falls out of a chute. He opens the door, takes out the piece of china, replaces it by the loaf and repeats the performance, so that the audience see that the mechanism is the crudest kind of false bottom. The second time he ends with the loaf in the machine and the piece of china in his hand. Then he puts back the dust sheet and wheels the machine backstage near Rakewell's sofa and takes up a position near Rakewell's head.

Recitative-Arioso-Recitative

RAKEWELL *(stirring in his sleep)*
       Oh I wish it were true.

SHADOW   Awake?

RAKEWELL *(starting up)*
         Who's there?

SHADOW   Your shadow, master.

RAKEWELL   You!
       O Nick, I've had the strangest dream. I thought —
       How could I know what I was never taught
       Or fancy objects I have never seen? —
       I had devised a marvellous machine,
       An engine that converted stones to bread
       Whereby all peoples were for nothing fed.

I saw all want abolished by my skill
And earth become an Eden of good will.

SHADOW (*with a conjuror's gesture, whipping the dust sheet off the machine*)
Did your machine look anything like this?

RAKEWELL I must be still asleep. That *is* my dream.

SHADOW How does it work?

RAKEWELL (*very excited*)
I need a stone.

SHADOW (*handing him the piece of vase*)
Try this.

RAKEWELL I place it here. I turn the wheel and then —
The bread!

The loaf falls out.

SHADOW (*Picking up the bread, he breaks off a piece and hands it to Rakewell.*)
Be certain. Taste!

RAKEWELL (*After tasting it, he falls on his knees.*)
O miracle!
Oh may I not, forgiven all my past
For one good deed, deserve dear Anne at last?

Duet   (*beside his machine, very elated and oblivious to his surroundings*)
[19]   Thanks to this excellent device
Man shall re-enter Paradise
   From which he once was driven.
Secure from need, the cause of crime,
The world shall for the second time
   Be similar to heaven.

SHADOW (*downstage; in a worldy-wise manner and taking the audience into his confidence*)
A word to all my friends, where'er you sit,
The men of sense, in boxes or the pit.
My master is a fool as you can see,
But you may do good business with me.

RAKEWELL When to his infinite relief
Toil, hunger, poverty and grief
   Have vanished like a dream,
This engine Adam shall excite
To hallelujahs of delight
   And ecstasy extreme.

SHADOW The idle drone and the deserving poor
Will give good money for this toy, be sure.
For, so it please, there's no fantastic lie
You cannot make men swallow if you try.

RAKEWELL Omnipotent when armed with this,
In secular abundant bliss
   He shall ascend the Chain
Of Being to its top to win
The throne of Nature and begin
   His everlasting reign.

SHADOW So, you who know your proper interest,
Here is your golden chance. Invest. Invest.
Come, take your shares immediately, my friends,
And praise the folly that pays dividends.

Recitative   Forgive me, master, for intruding upon your transports; but your dream is still a long way from fulfilment. Here is the machine, it is true. But it must be manufactured in great quantities. It must be advertised, it must be sold. We shall need money and advice. We shall need partners, merchants of probity and reputation in the City.

RAKEWELL   Alas, good Shadow, your admonitions are only too just; and they chill my spirit. For how am I, who am become a byword for extravagance and folly, to approach such men? Is this dream, too, this noble vision, to prove as empty as the rest? What shall I do?

SHADOW   Have no fear, master. Leave such matters to me. Indeed, I have already spoken with several notable citizens concerning your invention; and they are as eager to see it as you to show.

RAKEWELL   Ingenious Shadow! How could I live without you? I cannot wait. Let's visit them immediately.

Rakewell and Shadow begin wheeling the machine out. Just as they reach the door, Shadow, who is pulling in front, turns.

SHADOW   Should you not tell the good news to your wife?

RAKEWELL   My wife? I have no wife. I've buried her. (*Exeunt.*)

Quick curtain.

Gail Gilmour as Baba the Turk in a production by Hans Neugeberger, Cologne, 1982. (photo: Paul Leclaire)

Act Three

Scene One. *The same as Act Two, scene three, except that everything is covered with cobwebs and dust. Baba is still seated motionless at the table, the wig over her head, also covered with cobwebs and dust. Afternoon. Spring. Before the curtain rises a great choral cry of* 'Ruin, Disaster, Shame,' *is heard from behind it. When the curtain rises two groups of the Crowd of Respectable Citizens are examining the objects. Two other groups enter as the scene progresses.*

Chorus

GROUP I   What curious phenomena are up today for sale.

GROUP II   What manner of remarkables.

GROUP III (*entering. In the door, horrified*)
                  What squalor!

GROUP I (*crowded around some object, admiringly*)
                  What detail!

GROUP IV (*entering*)
                  I *am* so glad I did not miss the auction.

GROUP II   So am I.

GROUP III   I can't begin admiring.

GROUP IV   Oh fantastic!

TUTTI   Let us buy!

Again the cry of 'Ruin, Disaster, Shame,' *is heard from offstage. The Crowd pauses in its examination, looks at each other, then comes forward and addresses the audience with hushed voices that barely conceal a tinge of complacency.*

CROWD   Blasted! Blasted! so many hopes of gain:
                  Hundreds of sober merchants are insane;
                  Widows have sold their mourning-clothes to eat;
                  Herds of pale orphans forage in the street;
                  Many a Duchess divested of gems;
                  Has crossed the dread Styx by way of the Thames.
                  Oh stricken, take heart in placing the blame —
They begin to disperse again into groups examining the objects.
                  Rakewell. Rakewell. Ruin. Disaster. Shame.

Enter Anne. She looks about quickly and then approaches the Crowd group by group.

ANNE   Do *you* know where Tom Rakewell is?

GROUP I   America. He fled.

GROUP II   Spontaneous combustion caught him hurrying. He's dead.

ANNE   Do *you* know what's become of him?

GROUP III   Tom Rakewell? How should we?

GROUP IV   He's Methodist.

GROUP III   He's Papist.

GROUP IV   He's converting Jewry.

ANNE   Can *no* one tell me where he is?

TUTTI   We're certain he's in debt;
                  They're after him, they're after him, and they will catch him yet.

ANNE (*aside*) I'll seek him in the house myself. (*Exit*).

GROUPS I AND II   I wonder at her quest.

GROUPS III AND IV
                  She's probably some silly girl he ruined like the rest.

94

They return to their examination unconcernedly. Then the door is flung open and Sellem enters with a great flurry followed by a few Servants who begin clearing space and setting up a dais.

SELLEM Aha!

CROWD He's here,
The auctioneer.

SELLEM (*to the Servants*)
No! Over there.
They begin nervously setting it up again in another spot.
Be quick. Take care.

CROWD (*to each other*)
Your bids prepare.
Be quick. Take care.
Sellem mounts the dais and bows.

SELLEM

Recitative Ladies, both fair and gracious: gentlemen: be all welcome to this miracle of, this most widely heralded of, this — I am sure you follow me — *ne plus ultra* of auctions. (*Pause*) Truly there is a divine balance in Nature: a thousand lose that a thousand may gain; and you who are the fortunate are not so only in yourselves, but also in being Nature's missionaries. You are her instruments for the restoration of that order we all so worship, and it is granted to, ah! so few of us to serve.

He bows again. Applause.
Let us proceed at once. Lots one and two: which cover all objects subsumed under the categories —animal, vegetable and mineral.

During the following Sellem is continually on the move, indulging in elaborate by-play, holding up objects; Servants are rushing on and off the dais with objects; the Crowd is eager and attentive.

Aria [20] Who hears me, knows me; knows me
A man with value; look at this — (*holding up the stuffed auk*)
What is it? — Wit
And Profit: no one, no one
Could fail to conquer, fail to charm,
Who had it by
To watch. And who could not be
A nimble planner, having this (*holding up a mounted fish*)
Before him? Bid
To get them, get them, hurry!
During the next seven lines various individuals and groups in the Crowd are bidding excitedly: 'one, two, three, five, etc.'.
La! come bid.
Hmm! come buy.
Aha! the auk.
Witty, lovely, wealthy. Poof! go high!
La! Some more.
Hmm! Come on.
Aha! the pike. (*Silent pause.*)

Bidding scene

SELLEM AND CROWD
Seven — eleven — fourteen — nineteen — twenty — twenty-three — going — at twenty-three — going — going — gone.

CROWD Hurrah! (*Pause.*)

Sellem's aria (continuing)

SELLEM (*holding up a marble bust*)

> Behold it, Roman, moral,
> The man who has it, has it
> Forever — yes! (*He holds up a palm branch.*)
> And holy, holy, curing
> The body, soul and spirit;
> A gift of — God's!
> And not to mention this or   (*holding up*
> The other, more and more and —   *various*
> So help me — more!   *objects*)
> Then bid, oh get them, hurry!

The crowd, during the next seven lines, bids as before.

> La! come bid.
> Hmm! come buy.
> Aha! the bust.
> Feel them, life eternal: Poof! go high!
> La! some more.
> Hmm! come on.
> Aha! the palm. (*Silent pause.*)

Bidding scene

SELLEM AND CROWD

> Fifteen — and a half — three quarters — sixteen — seventeen — **going at**
> seventeen — going — going — gone.

CROWD   Hurrah! (*Pause.*)

Recitative

SELLEM   Wonderful. Yes, yes. And now for the truly adventurous —
(*walking over slowly to the covered Baba, and changing his voice to a suggestive whisper*)

Sellem's aria An unknown object draws us, draws us near.
(*continued*)   A cake? An organ? Golden Apple Tree?
> A block of copal? Mint of Alchemy?
> Oracle? Pillar? Octopus? Who'll see?
> Be brave! — Perhaps an angel will appear. (*Pause for effect.*)

During the next seven lines the Crowd bids as before, but this time get so excited that they almost drown out Sellem, and they begin fighting among themselves.

> La! come bid.
> Hmm! come buy.
> Aha! the it.
> This may be salvation. Poof! go high!
> La! be calm.
> Hmm! come on.
> Aha! the what.

At this point the Crowd is so raucous that Sellem is practically shouting by the time he ends the next phrase.

Final bidding scene

SELLEM AND CROWD

> Fifty — fifty-five — sixty — sixty-one — sixty-two — seventy — ninety —
> going at ninety — going at a hundred — going — going — gone.

In order to quiet the Crowd, Sellem, as he shouts his last 'Gone', snatches the wig off Baba's head. The effect quiets them immediately and she, for the moment completely impervious to her surroundings, finishes the word [cadenza] *she began in the last scene.*

BABA   (ne) . . . ver.

Then she looks quickly around, snatches up a veil that is lying on the table, stands up indignantly and during the next verse brushes herself off while the Crowd and Sellem murmur in the background over and over.

CROWD AND SELLEM
     It's Baba, his wife. It passes believing.

Aria

BABA
     Sold! Annoyed! I've caught you! — thieving!
       If you dare
       Touch a thing,
       Then beware
       My reckoning.
     Be off, be gone, desist:
     I, Baba, must insist
       Upon — your leaving.

The voices of Rakewell and Shadow are heard giving a street-cry from off stage.

RAKEWELL AND SHADOW
     Old wives for sale, old wives for sale!
     Stale wives, prim wives, silly and grim wives!
       Old wives for sale!

Recitative

SELLEM AND CROWD
     Now what was that?

BABA (*aside*)   The pigs of plunder!

Enter Anne hurriedly. She rushes to the window.

ANNE   Was that his voice?

SELLEM AND CROWD   What next, I wonder?

BABA (*aside*) The milk-maid taunts me.

ANNE (*at the window*)
          Gone!

BABA (*reflectively — after glancing about*)
               All I possessed
    Seems gone. (*shrugging her shoulders*)
        Well, well. (*to Anne, a bit imperiously and indulgently*)
          My dear!

ANNE (*turning*)
          His wife!

BABA   His jest —
    No matter now. Come here, my child, to Baba. (*Anne goes over to her.*)

SELLEM (*obviously under a strain*)
     Ladies, the sale, if you could go out.

BABA (*impatiently*)   Robber.
     Don't interrupt.

CROWD (*to him as he walks desperately to a corner of the room*)
          Don't interrupt or rail;

A SOLO VOICE
     A scene like this is better than a sale.

Duet [21]

BABA (*to Anne*)
     You love him, seek to set him right:
     He's but a shuttle-headed lad:
     Not quite a gentleman, nor quite
     Completely vanquished by the bad:
     Who knows what care and love might do?
     But good or bad, I know he still loves you.

ANNE	He loves me still! Then I alone
	In weeping doubt have been untrue.
	O hope, endear my love, atone,
	Enlighten, grace whatever may ensue.

SELLEM AND GROUPS I AND II
He loves her.

GROUPS III AND IV
Who?

SELLEM AND GROUPS I AND II
That isn't known.

GROUPS III AND IV
He loves her still.

SELLEM AND GROUPS I AND II
The tale is sad —

GROUPS III AND IV
— if true.

BABA	So find him, and his man beware!
	I may have made a bad mistake
	Yet I can tell who in that pair
	Is poisoned victim and who snake!
	Then go —

ANNE But where shall you — ?

BABA (*lifting her hand to interrupt gently*)
My dear,
A gifted lady never need have fear.
I shall go back and grace the stage,
Where manner rules and wealth attends. (*with an all-inclusive gesture*)
Can I deny my time its rage?
My self-indulgent intermezzo ends.

| ANNE | Can I for him all love engage |
| | And yet believe her happy when love ends? |

GROUPS III AND IV
She will go back.

GROUPS I AND II
Her view is sage.

GROUPS III AND IV
That's life.

GROUPS I AND II
We came to buy.

TUTTI See how it ends.

SELLEM (*despondently*)
Money farewell. Who'll buy? The auction ends.

At the end of the ensemble, the voices of Rakewell and Shadow are again heard from the street. All on stage pause to listen.

Ballad Tune

RAKEWELL AND SHADOW (*off stage*)
If boys had wings and girls had stings
And gold fell from the sky,
If new-laid eggs wore wooden legs
I should not laugh or cry.

ANNE It's Tom, I know!

BABA The two, then go!

SELLEM AND CROWD
The thief, below!

Stretto-Finale [22]

ANNE   I go to him.
         O love, be brave,
         Be swift, be true,
         Be strong for him and save.

BABA   Then go to him.
         In love be brave,
         Be swift, be true,
         Be strong for him and save.

SELLEM AND CROWD
         They're after him.
         His crime was grave;
         Be swift if you
         Want time enough to save.

ANNE (*pausing for a moment — to Baba*)
         May God bless you.

ALL (*but Anne*)
         Be swift if you
         Want time enough to save.

Anne rushes out. The voices of Rakewell and Shadow are heard disappearing in the distance.

Ballad tune (reprise)

RAKEWELL AND SHADOW
         Who cares a fig for Tory or Whig
           Not I, not I, not I.

Pause, then Baba turns and addresses Sellem with lofty command.

BABA   You! Summon my carriage!
He, impressed in spite of himself and certainly forgetting he came to auction off her carriage, bows, goes to the door and opens it for her. Baba addresses the Crowd:
         Out of my way!
Crowd falls back and she starts to leave — turning at the door, she pauses to remark:
         The next time *you* see Baba you shall pay.

Grand exit of Baba

CROWD (*murmuring*)
         I've never been through such a hectic day.

               Curtain.

Scene Two. *A starless night. A churchyard. Tombs. Front centre a newly-dug grave. Behind it a flat raised tomb, against which is leaning a sexton's spade. On the right a yew tree.*

Prelude

Enter Rakewell and Shadow left, the former out of breath, the latter carrying a little black bag.

Duet [23]

RAKEWELL How dark and dreadful is this place.
         Why have you led me here?
       There's something, Shadow, in your face
         That fills my soul with fear!

SHADOW   A year and a day have passed away
         Since first to you I came.
       All things you bid, I duly did
         And now my wages claim.

RAKEWELL   Shadow, good Shadow, be patient; I
           Am beggared, as you know,
           But promise when I am rich again
           To pay you all I owe.

SHADOW   'Tis not your money but your soul
           Which I this night require.
           Look in my eyes and recognise
           Whom — Fool! you chose to hire.

pointing out grave and taking the objects mentioned out of his bag
           Behold your waiting grave, behold
           Steel, halter, poison, gun.
           Make no excuse, your exit choose:
           Tom Rakewell's race is run.

RAKEWELL   Oh let the wild hills cover me
           Or the abounding wave.

SHADOW   The sins you did may not be hid.
           Think not your soul to save.

RAKEWELL   Oh why did an uncle I never knew
           Select me for his heir?

SHADOW   It pleases well the damned in Hell
           To bring another there.

           Midnight is come: by rope or gun
           Or medicine or knife,
           On the stroke of twelve you shall slay yourself
           For forfeit is your life.

A clock begins to strike.
           Count one, count two, count three, count four,
           Count five and six and seven.

RAKEWELL   Have mercy on me, Heaven.

SHADOW   Count eight —

RAKEWELL   Too late.

SHADOW   No wait.
He holds up his hand and the clock stops after the ninth stroke.

Recitative. Urbanely: Very well then, my dear and good Tom, perhaps you impose a bit
           upon our friendship; but Nick, as you know, is a gentleman at heart,
           forgives your dilatoriness and suggests — a game.

RAKEWELL   A game?

SHADOW   A game of chance [to] finally decide your fate. Have you a pack of cards?

RAKEWELL   *(taking a pack from his pocket)*
           All that remains me of this world — and for the next.

SHADOW   You jest. Fine, fine. Good spirits make a game go well. I shall explain. The
           rules are simple and the result simpler still: Nick will cut three cards. If you
           can name them, you are free; if not, *(He points to the instruments of death.)*
           you choose the path to follow me. You understand? *(Rakewell nods.)*
           Let us begin.

*Shadow shuffles the cards, places the pack in the palm of his left hand and cuts with his right,
holding then the portion with the exposed card towards the audience and away from Rakewell.*

Duet [24] Well, then.

RAKEWELL   My heart is wild with fear, my throat is dry,
           I cannot think, I dare not wish.

SHADOW   Come, try.
Let wish be thought and think on one to name,
You wish in all your fear could rule the game
Instead of Shadow.

RAKEWELL (*aside*)   Anne! (*silent pause, calmly*) My fear departs;
I name — the Queen of Hearts.

SHADOW (*holding up the card towards Rakewell*)
The Queen of Hearts.
He tosses it to one side. The clock strikes once.
You see, it's quite a simple game.
As Rakewell lifts his head in silent thanks, Shadow addresses the audience.
To win at once in love or cards is dull;
The gentleman loves sport, for sport is rare;
   The positive appalls him.
He plays the pence of hope to yield the guineas of despair.
turning back to Rakewell
Again, good Tom. You are my master yet.
He repeats the routine of shuffling and cutting the cards.

RAKEWELL What shall I trust in now? How throw the die
To win my soul back for myself?

SHADOW   Come, try.
Was Fortune not your mistress once? Be fair.
Give her at least the second chance to bare
The hand of Shadow.

The spade falls forward with a great crash.

RAKEWELL (*startled, cursing*)
                                                  The deuce!
Silent pause. Rakewell looks at what fell calmly.
                                                  She lights the shades
And shows — the two of spades.

SHADOW (*with scarcely contained anger throwing the card aside*)
                                                  The two of spades.
The clock strikes once.
Congratulations. The Goddess still is faithful.
Changing his tone.
But we have one more, you know, the very last. Think for a while, my Tom,
where you have come to. I would not want your last of chances thoughtless.
I am, you may have oftentimes observed, really compassionate. Think on
your hopes.

RAKEWELL Oh God, what hopes have I?

*He buries his face in his arm and leans against the tomb. Shadow reaches deftly down, picks up
one of the discarded cards and holds it up while he addresses the audience.*

SHADOW   The simpler the trick, the simpler the deceit;
That there is no return, I've taught him well,
   And repetition palls him;
The Queen of Hearts again shall be for him the Queen of Hell.
He slips the card into the pack and then turns to Rakewell.
Rouse yourself, Tom, your travail soon will end.
Routine with cards.
Come, try.
Pause.

RAKEWELL   Now in his words I find no aid.
Will Fortune give another sign?

101

SHADOW (*aside*)
>Now in my words he'll find no aid
>And Fortune gives no other sign.

Pause. Rakewell looks nervously about him.

SHADOW   Afraid,
>Love-lucky Tom? Come, try.

RAKEWELL (*frightened, looking away from the ground*)
>Dear God, a track of cloven hooves.

SHADOW (*sardonic*)
>The knavish goats are back
>To crop the spring's return.

RAKEWELL (*stepping forward, agonized*)
>Return! and Love!
>The banished words torment.

SHADOW   You cannot now repent.

RAKEWELL   Return O love —

ANNE (*off stage*)
>A love that is sworn before Thee can plunder Hell of its prey.

Rakewell, on recognizing Anne's voice, has broken off, amazed. Shadow stands as though frozen.

RAKEWELL (*spoken*)
>I wish for nothing else.
(*exalted*)   Love, first and last, assume eternal reign;
>Renew my life, O Queen of Hearts, again.

As he sings 'O Queen of Hearts, again' he snatches the exposed half-pack from the still motionless Shadow. The twelfth stroke sounds. With a cry of joy Rakewell sinks to the ground senseless.

SHADOW   I burn! I freeze! In shame I hear
>My famished legions roar;
>My own delay lost me my prey
>And damns myself the more.

>Defeated, mocked, again I sink
>In ice and flame to lie,
>But Heaven's will I'll hate and till
>Eternity defy.

looking at Rakewell
>Your sins, my foe, before I go
>Give me some power to pain:

with a magic gesture
>To reason blind shall be your mind
>Henceforth be you insane!

Slowly Shadow sinks into the grave. Blackout. The dawn comes up. It is spring. The open grave is now covered with a green mound upon which Rakewell sits smiling, putting grass on his head and singing to himself in a childlike voice.

RAKEWELL   With roses crowned, I sit on ground;
>Adonis is my name;
>The only dear of Venus fair;
>Methinks it is no shame.

Slow curtain.

Scene Three. *Bedlam. Backstage centre on a raised eminence a straw pallet. Rakewell stands before it facing the chorus of Madmen who include a blind man with a broken fiddle, a crippled soldier, a man with a telescope and three old hags.*

Arioso

RAKEWELL   Prepare yourselves, heroic shades. Wash you and make you clean. Anoint your limbs with oil, put on your wedding garments and crown your heads with flowers. Let music strike. Venus, queen of love, will visit her unworthy Adonis.

Dialogue

CHORUS   Madmen's words are all untrue;
She will never come to you.

RAKEWELL   She gave me her promise.

CHORUS   Madness cancels every vow;
She will never keep it now.

RAKEWELL   Come quickly, Venus, or I die.

He sits down on the pallet and buries his face in his hands. The Chorus dance before him with mocking gestures.

Chorus-Minuet [25]

CHORUS   Leave all love and hope behind;
Out of sight is out of mind
In these caverns of the dead.
In the city overhead
Former lover, former foe
To their works and pleasures go
Nor consider who beneath
Weep and howl and gnash their teeth.
Down in Hell as up in Heaven
No hands are in marriage given,
Nor is honour or degree
Known in our society.
Banker, beggar, whore and wit
In a common darkness sit.
Seasons, fashions, never change;
All is stale yet all is strange;
All are foes, and none are friends
In a night that never ends.

The sound of a key being turned in a rusty lock is heard.
Hark! Minos comes who cruel is and strong:
Beware! Away! His whip is keen and long.

They scatter to their cells. Enter Keeper and Anne.

Recitative

KEEPER (*pointing to Rakewell, who has not raised his head*)
There he is. Have no fear. He is not dangerous.

ANNE   Tom!

Rakewell still does not stir.

KEEPER   He believes that he is Adonis and will answer to no other name. Humour him in that, and you will find him easy to manage. So, as you desire, I'll leave you.

ANNE (*giving him money*) You are kind.

KEEPER   I thank you, Lady.

Exit Keeper. Anne goes up and stands close to Rakewell, who still has not moved. A moment's pause.

ANNE (*softly*) Adonis.

RAKEWELL (*raising his head and springing to his feet*) Venus, my queen, my bride. At last. I have waited for thee so long, till I almost believed those madmen who blasphemed against thy honour. They are rebuked. Mount, Venus, mount thy throne.

He leads her to the pallet on which she sits. He kneels at her feet.
O merciful goddess, hear the confession of my sins.

Duet [26]   In a foolish dream, in a gloomy labyrinth
I hunted shadows, disdaining thy true love;
Forgive thy servant, who repents his madness,
Forgive Adonis and he shall faithful prove.

ANNE (*rising and raising him by the hand*)
What should I forgive? Thy ravishing penitence
Blesses me, dear heart, and brightens all the past.
Kiss me Adonis: the wild boar is vanquished.

RAKEWELL Embrace me, Venus: I've come home at last.

RAKEWELL AND ANNE
Rejoice, beloved: in these fields of Elysium
Space cannot alter, nor Time our love abate:
Here has no words for absence or estrangement
Nor Now a notion of Almost or Too Late.

Rakewell suddenly staggers. Anne helps him gently to lie down on the pallet.

Recitative (*quasi arioso*)

RAKEWELL I am exceeding weary. Immortal queen, permit thy mortal bridegroom to lay his head upon thy breast.

He does so. The Heavens are merciful, and all is well. Sing, my beloved, sing me to sleep.

Lullaby [27]

ANNE   Gently, little boat
Across the ocean float,
The crystal waves dividing:
   The sun in the west
   Is going to rest;
      Glide, glide, glide
Toward the Islands of the Blest.

CHORUS (*off in their cells*)
What voice is this? What heavenly strains
Bring solace to tormented brains?

ANNE   Orchards greenly grace
That undisturbèd place,
The weary soul recalling
   To slumber and dream,
   While many a stream
      Falls, falls, falls,
Descanting on a childlike theme.

CHORUS   O sacred music of the spheres!
Where are our rages and our fears?

ANNE   Lion, lamb and deer,
Untouched by greed or fear
About the woods are straying:
   And quietly now
   The blossoming bough
      Sways, sways, sways
Above the fair unclouded brow.

CHORUS   Sing on! Forever sing! Release
Our frantic souls and bring us peace!

Enter Keeper with Trulove.

Recitative

TRULOVE   Anne, my dear, the tale is ended now.
Come home.

ANNE   Yes Father.
to Rakewell   Tom, my vow
Holds ever, but it is no longer I
You need. Sleep well, my dearest dear. Good-bye.

Anne comes down stage and joins Trulove.

Duettino

ANNE   Every wearied body must
Late or soon return to dust,
Set the frantic spirit free.
In this earthly city we
Shall not meet again, love, yet
Never think that I forget.

TRULOVE   God is merciful and just,
Good ordains what ought to be,
But a father's eyes are wet.

Exeunt Anne and Trulove and Keeper. A short pause. Then Rakewell wakes, starts to his feet and looks wildly around.

Finale (recitative and chorus)

RAKEWELL   Where art thou, Venus? Venus, where art thou? The flowers open to the sun. The birds renew their song. It is spring. The bridal couch is prepared. Come quickly, beloved, and we will celebrate the holy rites of love.
A moment's silence. Then shouting:
Holla! Achilles, Helen, Eurydice, Orpheus, Persephone,* all my courtiers. Holla!
The Chorus enter from all sides.
Where is my Venus? Why have you stolen her while I slept! Madmen! Where have you hidden her?

CHORUS   Venus? Stolen? Hidden? Where?
Madman! No one has been here.

RAKEWELL   My heart breaks. I feel the chill of death's approaching wing. Orpheus, strike from thy lyre a swan-like music, and weep, ye nymphs and shepherds of these Stygian fields, weep for Adonis the beautiful, the young; weep for Adonis whom Venus loved.

He falls back on the pallet.

Mourning Chorus

CHORUS   Mourn for Adonis, ever young, Venus' dear,
Weep, tread softly round his bier.

Slow curtain.

---

*also 'Plato' in the libretto, but not the score.

Epilogue

Before the curtain. House lights up. Enter Baba, Rakewell, Shadow, Anne, Trulove — the men without wigs, Baba without her beard.

ALL   Good people, just a moment:
     Though our story now is ended,
       There's the moral to draw
       From what you saw
     Since the curtain first ascended.

ANNE   Not every rake is rescued
     At the last by Love and Beauty;
       Not every man
       Is given an Anne
     To take the place of Duty.

BABA   Let Baba warn the ladies:
     You will find out soon or later
       That, good or bad,
       All men are mad;
     All they say or do is theatre.

RAKEWELL   Beware, young men who fancy
     You are Virgil or Julius Caesar,
       Lest when you wake
       You be only a rake.

TRULOVE   I heartily agree, sir!

SHADOW   Day in, day out, poor Shadow
     Must do as he is bidden.
       Many insist
       I do not exist.
     At times I wish I didn't.

ALL   So let us sing as one.
     At all times in all lands
     Beneath the moon and sun,
     This proverb has proved true
     Since Eve went out with Adam:
       For idle hands
       And hearts and minds
       The Devil finds
       A work to do,
     A work, dear Sir, fair Madam,
       For you and you.

Bow and exeunt.

               Finis.

Elsie Morison (Anne) and Alexander Young (Tom) at Sadler's Wells, 1962. (photo: Reg Wilson)

'For idle hearts and hands and minds the Devil finds a work to do.' The Epilogue in the Hockney-designed, Hogarth-inspired production with Felicity Lott (Anne), Leo Goeke (Tom), Katherine Pring (Baba), John Michael Flanagan (Trulove) and Samuel Ramey (Nick) at Glyndebourne, 1978. (photo: Guy Gravett)

The 1958 Prologue
W. H. Auden and Chester Kallman

In 1958 BBC television broadcast the last five scenes of the opera from Glyndebourne, and this prologue was written for Nick Shadow (played by Otakar Kraus) to introduce the action so far. We are most grateful to his son, Charles Kraus, for drawing our attention to this curiosity, and to Edward Mendelson, on behalf of The Estate of W. H. Auden, for allowing us to publish it here for the first time. The lines in square brackets were not actually spoken.

'I wish that I had money?' so Tom said.
He'll wish he'd wished for nothing soon instead!
Tom is Tom Rakewell, my new master's name,
Who knows me as Nick Shadow since I came
To serve his wishes. Well, well, he will learn
I've other titles when I wish in turn.
Imagine him before my part began,
A handsome, lazy, penniless young man,
Engaged — how I detest her! — to his sweetheart, Anne.
He loved her but he loved himself still more,
Life without pain was what he asked me for.
I hear his prayer; immediately I flew
To tell him that his First Wish had come true;
An unknown uncle who had died of late
Had made him sole heir to a vast estate.
Lucky for Tom? Poor fool! The luck was mine.
I knew at once I had him on my line,
For in his heart I read his secret thought —
'Twas not of love, but pleasures to be bought.
To town I led him, there to introduce
My panting victim to kind Mother Goose.
What followed, you can guess: to my mind, whoring
And drunkenness and cards are vastly boring.
Tom's nature, though, I'm glad to say, proved such
That nature's pleasures did not please him much:
[The noise and glitter soon began to pall,
The ruling senses made no sense at all,]
Then, feeling nature but a foolish trap, he
Leaned back and sighed — 'I wish that I were happy!',
And I, at once, was at his side once more,
His wish to grant and my wish to assure.
'The happy man', I said, 'behaves in spite
Of custom, conscience, reason, appetite.
So, master, with your happiness in mind
Look on this portrait of strange womankind
— Baba the Turk — unrivalled anywhere,
The present wonder of St Giles' Fair.
Marry her, Tom! Be happy and rejoice,
Knowing you know no motive for your choice.
Think, Tom! Dare any marry her but you?'
He looked. He thought. He laughed. He went to woo.
Perhaps you ask, dear viewers, how this man
Could think of marriage and not think of Anne
Who is, I grant, a lovely loving She,
While Baba, to be candid, is — you'll see.
[He thought of her and felt ashamed, but pride

108

Richard Lewis (Tom) and Elsie Morison (Anne) in August 1958. (photo: BBC)

Soon won his guilty conscience to my side;
The Tom of his reproaches is not weak
But wicked, unforgiveable, unique.]
So to our play. The wedding-knot is tied,
And here you'll meet the bridegroom and the bride.
Too soon will Hymen's bed be full of lumps,
Baba in tears, and young Tom in the dumps.
What will his third wish be? All men are much the same;
Abused at home, they wish for public fame.
What road to ruin shall I then suggest?
Some business venture will, I think, be best.
Ruin... Despair... then... ah! one seeming-clever
Immortal soul called Tom is mine for ever.
[But here the couple come... No?... It is Anne!
Praying that Heaven will defeat my plan.
So — damn her! — let her pray! Nick Shadow knows his man.]

Selective Discography
David Nice

Oedipus Rex fared well on record during the 1960s and 70s, but compact discs have been slow to catch up. Colin Davis made two recordings, of which the 1983 version (perhaps too plushy for the spirit of the piece) boasts the imperious Jocasta of Jessye Norman, with Thomas Moser as Oedipus and Michel Piccoli as the Speaker (Orfeo 1071-831; also on cassette). Solti's 1976 performance (Decca CD only, 430 001-2) has the veteran Peter Pears struggling with the rich, melismatic writing of Oedipus's earlier scenes, though supremely moving in 'Invidia fortunam' and 'Lux facta est'. His earlier contribution, on the first of Stravinsky's own recordings (1951), is a better all-round performance; it is currently unavailable. Stravinsky's 1963 performance is due for CD release in the Stravinsky Edition from Sony Classics. Also to be reissued are Davis's other recording, an early Ansermet performance with Ernst Haefliger (an ideally lyrical Oedipus) and Bernstein's 1976 version. One outstanding live recording on CD comes from Claudio Abbado and the RAI orchestra and chorus (Memories, HR 4128), with Lajos Kozma and Tatiana Troyanos. A glimpse of Stravinsky conducting is a live recording of the celebrated 1952 Théâtre des Champs-Elysées cast, with a restrained *bel canto* Oedipus (Léopold Simoneau) and Cocteau as the Speaker (Disques Montaigne TCE 8760), a two-CD set with *Scènes de ballet* conducted by Stravinsky, and *Le Rossignol* conducted by André Cluytens. The fever-pitch of the opera's later scenes may surprise anyone who thinks of Stravinsky as a calmly austere conductor.

There are two recordings of Stravinsky conducting *The Rake's Progress* — in 1953 with the Metropolitan Opera, and in 1964 with the Royal Philharmonic Orchestra (and Sadler's Wells chorus) — but neither is currently available. The 1964 version is scheduled for CD issue by Sony Classics in 1991. Recommended for documentary value and expressive conducting, they can hardly match the orchestral pungency of the London Sinfonietta under Riccardo Chailly on Decca's 1984 recording (two CDs, Decca 411 644-2). On the other hand this diverges quite frequently from the score's (fairly strict) metronome indications, especially in the slower numbers. For instance, to hear Anne's Act One aria take wing you have to turn to Dawn Upshaw's recital disc (Elektra Nonesuch 7559-79187-2), where David Zinman's Orchestra of St Luke's lends close-balanced, characterful support for Upshaw's exceptionally intelligent interpretation of the text. It was bold of Decca to cast the young Cathryn Pope as Anne — more reticent than Upshaw, she shows every sign of promise as a recording artist in her few moments of confidence; there are strong performances from Philip Langridge as Tom and Samuel Ramey as Nick, and a magnificent Baba from Sarah Walker. For devotees of the Hockney designs, the Glyndebourne production is available on video (Pickwick SL2008), conducted by Haitink, with Samuel Ramey, Leo Goeke and Felicity Lott.

Bibliography

Among the numerous books of Stravinskiana edited, compiled or written by Robert Craft which include chapters about these operas, the *Selected Correspondence* is of outstanding importance. Volume I (Faber, 1982) contains the correspondence with Cocteau and with Auden. Volume III, Appendix D, (Faber, 1985) has a fascinating survey of the stage history of *Oedipus Rex*, describing the first productions in Vienna (designed by Roller) and Berlin (at the Kroll, conducted by Klemperer, designed by Dülberg), taken from an exhibition review. Also by Craft, *Dialogues and A Diary* (Doubleday, 1963; Faber, 1968) features a dialogue about *Oedipus* ('A Greek Trilogy') and 'Letters on *Oedipus Rex* (1925-27)', but it also includes the immensely enjoyable first-hand account of Robert Craft's diary 1948-62, in which he records (*inter alia*) meetings with Auden over *The Rake* in 1948, and with Ingmar Bergman for the 1961 production of that opera in Stockholm. The draft scenario of *The Rake* resulting from the 1947 Hollywood meeting is reprinted as Appendix C in Craft's *Memories and Commentaries* (Doubleday, 1960; Faber, 1960), while Stravinsky's 1964 programme note on *The Rake* and Vera Stravinsky's memoir of 'la prima assoluta' in 1951 are to be found in her *Themes and Conclusions* (Faber, 1972). Craft also has an essay in the Cambridge Opera Handbook by Paul Griffiths to *The Rake's Progress*, a useful introduction to the opera (1982).

Eric Walter White, *Stravinsky: The Composer and His Works* (Faber 1966, second edition 1979), remains a basic work of reference. There are two general books about Stravinsky which are well worth attention, Robert Craft's *Stravinsky: Chronicle of a Friendship, 1948-1971* (Knopf/Gollancz, 1972) and *Stravinsky in Pictures and Documents* (Hutchinson, 1979) by Craft and Vera Stravinsky.

Jean Cocteau writes about *Oedipus Rex* in *Journal d'un inconnu* (Grasset, 1953); it was translated as *The Hand of a Stranger*, by Alec Brown (Calder, 1956). A standard biography of Jean Cocteau, which includes details of *Oedipus Rex*, is Francis Steegmuller, *Cocteau: A Biography* (Macmillan, 1970), as does Frederick Brown, *An Impersonation of Angels: A Biography of Jean Cocteau* (Longmans, 1969). *Jean Cocteau and his World* (Thames and Hudson, 1987) by King Peters is an account of Cocteau's theatre. His four-act play *La Machine infernale*, 1934 (*The Infernal Machine*, trans. Carl Wildman, 1936, Oxford), is a re-working of the Oedipus material, strongly influenced by *Hamlet*, while his play, *Oedipe-Roi* — a longer version of the text which Stravinsky set — exists separately but is not translated.

As for the Auden connection, Roger Savage recommends Part Two of Humphrey Carpenter's biography of *W. H. Auden* (George Allen & Unwin, 1981), and chapters III and IV of *The Poetry of W. H. Auden: The Disenchanted Island* (Oxford, 1963) by Monroe K. Spears. A lecture on opera, 'The World of Opera', is the third in Auden's *Secondary Worlds* (Faber, 1968). For Kallman and the Auden-Kallman relationship, see Dorothy J. Farnan's *Auden in Love* (Simon and Schuster, 1984). All the Auden-Kallman libretti are due to be published in the second of the four volumes of the *Complete Works of W. H. Auden*, edited by Edward Mendelson, and is eagerly awaited. There is a good piece on Auden and *The Rake's Progress* by Robert Craft ('The Poet and the Rake') in *W. H. Auden: A Tribute* (Weidenfeld and Nicolson, 1975), edited by Stephen Spender. One of the best discussions of Hogarth is to be found in *Hogarth: The Complete Catalogue* by Joseph Burke and Colin Caldwell (Thames and Hudson, 1968).

Laelia Goehr's photograph of Stravinsky, which is reproduced on the cover, is one of many magnificent images included in her *Musicians in Camera* (Bloomsbury, 1989).

Contributors

David Nice, freelance journalist and broadcaster, is the author of a forthcoming book on *The Operas of Richard Strauss* (Octopus, London).

Judith Weir is the composer of two operas (*A Night at the Chinese Opera* and *The Vanishing Bridegroom*), and the ballet *Heaven Ablaze*. She has a commission to write an opera for ENO.

Roger Savage is a Senior Lecturer in English Literature at Edinburgh University, whose interests range from Purcell's semi-operas to Indian ragas. He has published several articles on seventeenth- and eighteenth-century music-theatre in *Early Music*, and produced *The Rake's Progress* for Edinburgh University Opera Club in 1987.

Brian Trowell is Heather Professor of Music at the University of Oxford, and produced the British stage première of *The Rake's Progress* in 1956, and the London stage première with the New Opera Company at Sadler's Wells in 1957.

Acknowledgements

Grateful acknowledgement is due to all those who have helped in the preparation of this book, notably Jennifer Batchelor, Anita Crowe and Charlotte Lowe. The Editor is also very grateful to Edward Mendelson for his comments on the libretto of *The Rake's Progress*.

Otakar Kraus (Nick) and Alexander Young (Tom) at Sadler's Wells, 1969. (photo: Reg Wilson)